TECHNICAL REPORT

Measuring the Effectiveness of Border Security Between Ports-of-Entry

Henry H. Willis • Joel B. Predd • Paul K. Davis • Wayne P. Brown

Sponsored by the Department of Homeland Security

RAND | HOMELAND SECURITY AND DEFENSE CENTER

This research was sponsored by the Department of Homeland Security and was conducted under the auspices of the Homeland Security and Defense Center, a joint center of the RAND National Security Research Division and RAND Infrastructure, Safety, and Environment.

Library of Congress Cataloging-in-Publication Data

Measuring the effectiveness of border security between ports- of-entry / Henry H. Willis ... [et al.].
       p. cm.
   Includes bibliographical references.
   ISBN 978-0-8330-4977-3 (pbk. : alk. paper)
   1. Border security—United States—Evaluation. 2. United States. Dept. of Homeland Security—Planning.
   3. Strategic planning—United States. I. Willis, Henry H.

   JV6483.M338 2010
   363.28'50684—dc22
                                                                                         2010013974

The RAND Corporation is a nonprofit research organization providing objective analysis and effective solutions that address the challenges facing the public and private sectors around the world. RAND's publications do not necessarily reflect the opinions of its research clients and sponsors.

RAND® is a registered trademark.

Published 2010 by the RAND Corporation
1776 Main Street, P.O. Box 2138, Santa Monica, CA 90407-2138
1200 South Hayes Street, Arlington, VA 22202-5050
4570 Fifth Avenue, Suite 600, Pittsburgh, PA 15213-2665
RAND URL: http://www.rand.org/
To order RAND documents or to obtain additional information, contact
Distribution Services: Telephone: (310) 451-7002;
Fax: (310) 451-6915; Email: order@rand.org

Preface

About This Report

The U.S. Department of Homeland Security (DHS) is responsible for securing the land, air, and maritime borders of the United States. Strategic planning is necessary if DHS is to do so effectively and efficiently. As part of that, DHS leadership must define concrete and sensible objectives and measures of success. These can be used to assess results along the way, to guide allocation of resources, and to inform programming and budgeting for future capabilities and functions.

To support these efforts, the DHS Office of Program Analysis and Evaluation asked the RAND Corporation for research and recommendations about strategic-level measures for assessing the effectiveness of border-security efforts and informing program decisions, which inevitably involve trade-offs within and across DHS missions. This report describes the results of a short study on such measures. It should be of interest to analysts and leaders responsible for establishing and implementing border-security policies and seeking to understand how to develop measures for the effectiveness of homeland security programs.

The RAND Homeland Security and Defense Center

This research was conducted under the auspices of the RAND Homeland Security and Defense Center, which conducts analysis to prepare and protect communities and critical infrastructure from natural disasters and terrorism. Center projects examine a wide range of risk management problems, including coastal and border security, emergency preparedness and response, defense support to civil authorities, transportation security, domestic intelligence programs, technology acquisition, and related topics. Center clients include the Department of Homeland Security, the Department of Defense, the Department of Justice, and other organizations charged with security and disaster preparedness, response, and recovery. The Homeland Security and Defense Center is a joint center of the RAND National Security Research Division and RAND Infrastructure, Safety, and Environment.

Questions or comments about this monograph should be sent to the project leader, Henry H. Willis (Henry_Willis@rand.org). Information about the Homeland Security and Defense Center is available online (http://www.rand.org/multi/homeland-security-and-defense/). Inquiries about homeland security research projects should be sent to:

Andrew Morral, Director
Homeland Security and Defense Center
RAND Corporation
1200 South Hayes Street
Arlington, VA 22202-5050
703-413-1100, x5119
Andrew_Morral@rand.org

Contents

Figures

Tables

Summary

Strategic planning is necessary if the U.S. Department of Homeland Security (DHS) is to carry out its border-security missions effectively and efficiently. As part of that, DHS leadership must define concrete and sensible objectives and measures of success. These can be used to assess results along the way, to guide allocation of resources, and to inform programming and budgeting for future capabilities and functions.

The U.S. Coast Guard (USCG), Customs and Border Protection (CBP), and Immigration and Customs Enforcement (ICE) have each developed measures to support their own operational planning and evaluation processes. Many of these measures are viewed by the DHS components to be useful for these purposes. However, the department is interested in continuing the development of its measures as a way to better inform its decisionmaking processes across the department. For instance, DHS has stated that CBP's measure of "miles of border under effective control" is in need of continued development in order to better evaluate border-security efforts in the land domain (DHS, 2008). USCG, in contrast, evaluates border control in the sea domain by measuring the probability of interdicting drugs and migrants, a method that could also be employed in the land domain. Thus, the DHS Office of Program Analysis and Evaluation asked RAND Corporation for research and recommendations on ways to measure the overall efforts of the national border-security enterprise between ports of entry.

Criteria For Good Measures

To be meaningful, the set of measures for effectiveness of border security should be

- *sound:* the measures reflect what is important
- *reliable:* the measures are easy to interpret and are difficult to manipulate
- *useful:* the measures can be feasibly monitored
- *general:* where possible, the measures can be broadly applied to DHS border-security efforts.

To identify measures that meet these criteria, we first developed a conceptual model of border phenomena. This reflected discussions with DHS component agencies engaged in border-security efforts, review of prior studies of border security, and field visits to the southwestern U.S. border during the past year.

A Conceptual Model of Border Security

DHS border-security missions are diverse and include efforts to prevent crime, maintain safety around borders, protect natural resources, and facilitate the legitimate movement of goods. All of these missions are important and enduring, but three missions appear to currently be of special interest to DHS leadership because they are especially problematic: illegal drug control, counterterrorism, and illegal migration. We treated these as "focus missions" in our study.

From examining each of them separately, we were led to a common conceptual model of how border-security efforts contribute to missions: essentially by controlling illegal flows, as indicated in Figure S.1.

As suggested by this model, we recommend measuring performance of three fundamental functions that border-security efforts contribute to achieving national policy objectives:

- *interdiction:* disrupting illegal movements across borders
- *deterrence:* convincing would-be smugglers, criminals, or terrorists not to attempt to illegally cross borders
- *exploiting networked intelligence:* contributing to and using shared intelligence information across organizational boundaries.

Measuring these functions requires specification of submeasures or indirect measures for each function. To measure interdiction, we recommend approximating interdiction rate by estimating the percentage of attempted flow that is nominally covered by border-security efforts (i.e., coverage) and the probability of interdiction for the flow that is covered. Reliable direct measurement of deterrence is not feasible, but deterrence is a real and important consequence of border-security effects on the decisions of would-be border crossers. Thus, we suggest measuring the quality of related efforts by the extent to which border-security agencies adhere to identified best practices for influencing decisions of smugglers, terrorists, and other criminals. Similarly, to measure networked intelligence, we recommend measuring the extent

Figure S.1
Conceptual Model of Border Security

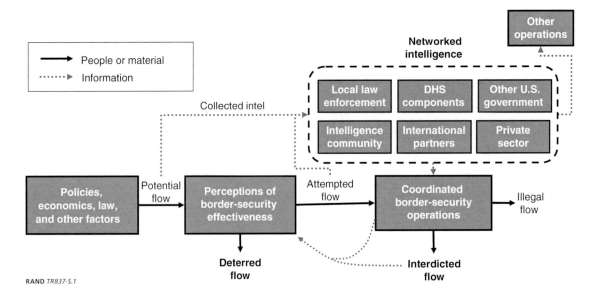

RAND *TR837-S.1*

to which border-security agencies adhere to identified best practices for collection, sharing, and exploitation of intelligence.

Finally, each of the three focus missions raises issues related to measurement and estimation of interdiction, deterrence, and networked intelligence. Table S.1 summarizes these issues, each of which is discussed further in the report.

Table S.1
Candidate Measures, Measurement Issues, and Approaches for Estimation

Objective	Measure	Submeasure or Indirect Measure	Measurement Issues and Approaches for Estimation
Interdict flow	Interdiction rate	Probability of interdiction for covered and lightly covered borders	• Where applicable, decompose into component probabilities (i.e., detect, respond, identify, and interdict). • Use empirical information (including red-team methods) and appropriately validated computer models to help support performance evaluation and planning.
		Coverage	• For terrorism, estimate subjectively the likelihood of terrorist intrusion efforts for lightly covered routes (with updates to reflect anticipated adaptations where shortcomings are observable). • For drug control, estimate the percentage of drug flow currently covered to nominal levels by border-security systems. • For illegal migration, estimate percentage of illegal migration covered to nominal levels by border-security systems. • For all, distinguish cases based on, e.g., terrain, relative knowledge, tactics.

Deter flow	Effects on border-crosser decisionmaking	Indirect measure: adherence to "best practices" for deterrence	• Best practices should reflect knowledge about deterring factors, such as
			  – probability of capture
			  – consequence of capture
			  – complexity of tactics required to succeed
			  – cost of necessary assets
			  – uncertainties
			  – availability of alternatives.
			• Importance of the factors will vary across missions, regions, and modes.
			• Decisionmakers must identify practices that are judged to have positive effects on outcomes.
			• These "best practices" should be routinely reviewed and updated and their value to improved outcomes estimated.
			• Adherence to "best practices" can be measured.
			• Program options can be assessed for value in permitting best practices.

Exploit networked intelligence	Effective collection, use, and sharing of intelligence	Indirect measure: adherence to best practices	• Best practices should reflect knowledge of DHS, intelligence, and law-enforcement communities. They should involve
			  – information collection (biographic, biometric, links)
			  – sharing with other agencies
			  – practiced cooperation with other agencies
			  – practiced operational use of networked intelligence.
			• Importance of practices may differ for drug control, counterterrorism, and illegal migration, and across regions and modes.
			• Decisionmakers must identify practices that are judged to have positive effects on outcomes.
			• These "best practices" should be routinely reviewed and updated and their value to improved outcomes estimated.
			• Adherence to "best practices" can be measured.
			• Program options can be assessed for value in permitting best practices.

Implementing Steps to Measure Border Security

To the extent that the conceptual model captures the essence of border security, the proposed measures for these functions are sound and reliable. Furthermore, application of these proposed measures to the three focus missions suggests that they can be generally applied to DHS border missions. However, practical implementation would require a number of steps.

A first step toward implementing this approach to measuring border security will be to understand how data that are currently collected by DHS map to the functions of interdicting illegal flows, deterring illegal flows, and exploiting networked intelligence. This could be the focus of a straightforward follow-on study.

Other steps will require more concerted analytic effort. These include the following:

- Develop a range of models to support planning (and performance evaluation, in some instances), primarily in the context of exploratory analysis under uncertainty.
- Identify and exploit opportunities to estimate attempted illegal crossings.
- Translate studies of adversary decisionmaking into doctrine for deterrence.
- Identify best practices for exploiting networked intelligence.
- Use layered portfolio-analysis methods to evaluate past or ongoing border-security efforts, to evaluate forward-looking border-security options to improve performance, and to relate results to the levels of success in other agencies' efforts.

If the steps described here are taken, DHS and its components will be in a better position to discuss past performance and to provide reasoned justifications for future allocation of resources. Furthermore, they will be able to relate their efforts to those of other agencies in pursuit of national objectives.

Acknowledgments

This study benefited from suggestions and guidance provided by numerous individuals at the Department of Homeland Security (DHS). The lead analyst responsible for guiding this study at DHS headquarters was Gregory Pejic. Throughout the effort, he provided valuable insights into related border-security measurement and planning efforts across the department. At DHS headquarters, we also thank Amy Culbertson, assistant director of performance management for the office of the chief financial officer, and John Whitley, director of the DHS Office of Program Analysis and Evaluation. Within Customs and Border Protection, we thank Alan Carr; Jennifer Chong; David Hoffman, deputy division chief; Anthony Holladay, assistant chief patrol agent; Merv Leavitt; Stephen Martin, deputy division chief; Gerald Martino; Julia Matthews; Jaime Salazar, patrol agent in charge; Teresa Smith; Carl Sublett; and Mickey Valdez, branch chief patrol agent. Within the Coast Guard, we thank CDR David Cooper, CPT Patrick De Quattro, LCDR Patrick Hilbert, LT Paul St. Pierre, and LCDR Eric Williams. Within Immigration Customs and Enforcement, we thank Gregory Archambeault, Richard Bak, Ken Heller (now of U.S. Citizenship and Immigration Services), Corey Katz, Christopher Lau, Mike Mendoza, Bill Rutten, Michael Tennyson, Christopher Tighe, and Elizabeth Williams. We also thank LTC Eloy Cuevas of the U.S. Army and Patrick Ryan of MicroSystems Integration for helpful discussions.

Whereas the discussions with these individuals contributed greatly to our understanding of the issues of securing the U.S. border, the views presented in this report are, of course, our responsibility.

Abbreviations

CBP	Customs and Border Protection
DHS	U.S. Department of Homeland Security
DoD	U.S. Department of Defense
FBI	Federal Bureau of Investigation
ICE	Immigration and Customs Enforcement
ONDCP	Office of National Drug Control Policy
USCG	U.S. Coast Guard

CHAPTER ONE

Introduction

Three U.S. Department of Homeland Security (DHS) component agencies carry out the majority of border-security missions: the U.S. Coast Guard (USCG), U.S. Customs and Border Protection (CBP), and Immigration and Customs Enforcement (ICE). The total effort expended each year by these agencies to secure borders exceeds $12 billion and involves construction of new infrastructure, acquisition of advanced surveillance technologies, and more than 60,000 officers, agents, pilots, civilians, and enlisted personnel (DHS, 2009a).

Strategic planning is necessary if the department is to carry out its border-security missions effectively and efficiently. Senior leadership must align DHS strategic planning with national strategies that rely on or affect border-security capabilities, communicate these strategic plans to other agencies and Congress, and advocate effectively for coherent cross-agency national functions of which border security is a part. As part of that, DHS leadership must define concrete and sensible objectives and measures of success. These can be used to assess results along the way, to guide allocation of resources, and to inform programming and budgeting for future capabilities and functions.

The USCG, CBP, and ICE have each developed measures to support their own operational planning and evaluation processes. Many of these measures are viewed by DHS components to be useful for these purposes. However, the department is interested in continuing the development of its measures as a way to better inform its decisionmaking processes across the department. For instance, DHS has stated that CBP's measure of "miles of border under effective control" is in need of continued development in order to better evaluate border-security efforts in the land domain (DHS, 2008). USCG, on the other hand, evaluates border control in the sea domain by measuring the probability of interdicting drugs and migrants, a method that could also be employed in the land domain. Thus, the DHS Office of Program Analysis and Evaluation asked RAND Corporation for research and recommendations on ways to measure the overall efforts of the national border-security enterprise between ports of entry.

This scoping excludes enforcement efforts at ports of entry and within the interior of the United States. The between-ports-of-entry border-control challenge, however, remains complex. It involves transit via air, land, and sea, and multiple component agencies. Moreover, it involves addressing numerous illegal or nefarious activities, including movements of drugs, weapons, money, and terrorists and other criminals. It also inevitably involves trade-offs within and across DHS missions.

The report proceeds as follows. Chapter Two reviews general DHS border-control missions, suggests a subset of "focus missions" of particular interest (drug control, counterterrorism, and illegal migration control), and discusses what constitutes good measures of effectiveness. Chapter Three describes a conceptual model that serves as a foundation for a discussion of measuring the effectiveness of border security, relates DHS-unique missions to larger national-level missions to which they are inextricably related, and highlights three core border-security functions to be measured (interdiction, deterrence, and intelligence networking). Chapter Four then applies the conceptual model to the focus missions described in Chapter Two. Chapter Five identifies hierarchies of measures and submeasures that are necessary when estimating the effectiveness of border security for the focus missions. Finally, Chapter Six discusses next steps toward integrating enriched versions of the suggested measures into planning and program evaluation.

General Missions, Focus Missions, and Criteria for Measuring Effectiveness

Our task includes sorting out what DHS's border-security efforts should accomplish, establishing measures that will be useful and meaningful, and connecting those efforts to other missions and to the efforts of other agencies within and outside DHS.

2.1 Understanding Related DHS Missions and Operations

Background research was crucial to developing recommendations for measuring the effectiveness of border-security efforts. It included (1) headquarters-level discussions of border security with the USCG, CBP, and ICE; (2) review of relevant past studies by government agencies, think tanks, and academics; and (3) field visits and observation of U.S. Border Patrol operations in the southwest region. Building on this research, we sought to synthesize what we had learned and then focus on a subset of issues for which useful suggestions could be made.

2.1.1 The Breadth of Enduring Missions

It is essential to recognize that DHS's component agencies have *many* enduring core missions that make headlines only when something extraordinary happens (e.g., a humanitarian rescue, an infringement of sovereignty, the spread of diseases or invasive species, or smuggling of special-purpose guns to criminal elements in Mexico that attack the Mexican police and army). The agencies are very sensitive to their obligations under the law to carry out these enduring missions consistently and well. They also know that doing so is much of what occupies them from day to day.

In contrast, policymakers often focus on currently relevant special issues for which there are known serious problems. They quite reasonably expect priority to be given to them when allocating resources. The component agencies are sympathetic and want to be responsive, but they correctly recognize that all of the core missions will continue. As a result, there can be some tension—a tension felt in our own study.

Both perspectives must be considered when defining measures of border-security effectiveness. Furthermore, it is important that the measures assist leadership in understanding why particular efforts are important to the nation, why a proposed portfolio balance is appropriate when allocating resources, and what components can be expected to accomplish. Even when much of the policy attention is on "focus missions," it is important to keep track of consequences for all of the enduring missions.

Figure 2.1
Decomposition of Objectives for Border Security Between Ports of Entry

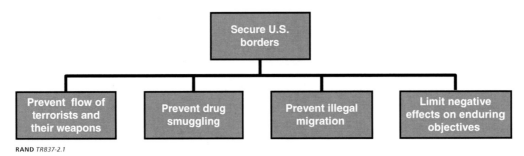

RAND *TR837-2.1*

Specifically, a challenge for planning is the potential for focus missions to pull resources inappropriately from each other or from other enduring missions. Although the other missions may be seen as acceptably managed now, decisions to draw resources away from them could lead to other problems in the future. This danger should be assessed as reflected in explicit measures rather than relegated to cautionary comments.

2.1.2 Focus Missions

With this recognition of the breadth of enduring missions generally, we identified three "focus missions" for special attention because of their current significance to top leadership: (1) illegal drug control, (2) counterterrorism, and (3) illegal migration control. Violence along the southwestern border related to the illegal drug trade has risen to intolerable levels and, at times, threatens to extend across the border into the United States. The threat of terrorists bringing nuclear materials, weapons, or terrorist operatives into the country is of great concern because of the potential for a catastrophic terrorist attack. Issues of illegal migration also continue to be of great concern to policymakers and the general public. Because policy analysis will be motivated by the search for solutions to these problems, measures of border security must address how border-security efforts contribute to solving these broader problems.

Figure 2.1 shows a high-level decomposition of the border-security mission that highlights the three focus objectives (lower row), but also includes the explicit objective of limiting negative effects on other enduring objectives.[1]

2.2   Framing Border Security within a System of Solutions to National Missions

One of our early conclusions was that it makes no sense to focus exclusively on DHS border-security efforts in isolation, because they are merely part of solutions to complex "system problems." One example is countering illegal drug use. The national policy instruments for controlling illegal drug use include aspects of public education, addiction treatment, laws and their enforcement, sentencing guidelines, diplomatic relations with source countries for drugs, *and* border security. Thus, achieving the ultimate goals of drug control certainly depends on

---

[1]   In a fuller treatment, the lower right box would refer also to achieving positives—i.e., actions taken in pursuit of the other objectives that have beneficial consequences for the other enduring missions. In practice, the greater concern is usually negative side effects, as when resources are drawn down excessively from the "other" missions or when efforts to prevent problems inhibit commerce and normal travel of citizens.

federal border-security capabilities, but it also depends on the effectiveness of other federal, state, and local agencies' work. Furthermore, assessment of any border-security capability must also account for potential side effects, such as economic costs, inconvenience to citizens, or relations with foreign neighbors.

To illustrate, border-security efforts can significantly raise the costs and risks to smugglers, perhaps reducing incentives for illegal drug trade. However, these border-security efforts will not be fully effective unless other agencies do their part to contribute to reducing the number of illegal drug users and establishing predictable and strict sentencing outcomes for those smugglers who are apprehended. This type of system view of border security can be applied to the other problems addressed in this study, such as preventing illegal migration, terrorism, or other cross-border criminal activity.

It follows that, in conceptualizing the border-security problem and developing measures of effectiveness, it is necessary to have an analytic system that accommodates national-level perspectives and what DHS-specific efforts contribute to solving the national-level problems.

2.3 Measuring Contributions to Border Security

Given that we have an understanding of general missions, focus missions, and relationships to national missions, how do we proceed to develop measures of performance? Such measures need to characterize outcomes that would be *expected* from border-security efforts and the risk that outcomes could be worse for a variety of reasons, including program failure, adversary adaptation, and erroneous analysis.[2] Before suggesting such measures, it is useful to summarize the principles that we used.

To be meaningful, the *set* of measures used by border security should be *sound*, *reliable*, *useful*, and (where possible) *general*. Let us define what these mean.[3]

Sound. To be sound, the measures should relate well to the actual phenomena occurring and be focused on the objectives being sought. Experience has shown that finding sound measures for complex systems, such as border security, requires a coherent conceptual understanding of the objectives that the system is designed to achieve, the dynamics of the phenomena that threaten those objectives, and how operational programs influence the threats to the objectives. Having such an underlying conceptual model is crucial to distinguishing between measures that are truly central to overall effectiveness and performance of component systems

---

[2] The word *risk* has many meanings. In most of this report, we use *risk* as the potential for worse-than-expected results (e.g., a program may fail to deliver, or predicted assessment of its effectiveness may be wrong). Others use the term *risk* differently. To illustrate, suppose that an organization has three missions (A, B, and C) and limited resources. Review might indicate that performance is falling short in A and B, whereas C is doing well. Resources might be reallocated so that acceptable results are *expected* in pursuit of A, B, and C. Some refer to that as *risk management*. In our terminology, we would refer to *allocating resources to achieve a balance of expected results* (i.e., mean results). We would then address the need for hedges against risk (i.e., against results being worse than expected). We occasionally use *risk* with yet another common meaning: danger to U.S. personnel or danger perceived by would-be border crossers.

[3] Different criteria are used in DHS training courses and by the U.S. Government Accountability Office, but in different contexts and for different purposes. The criteria listed are often more numerous and include a mixture of fundamental attributes and attributes related to administration and management. We found it necessary to use our own, although establishing that we could map among sets of criteria. Ours are philosophically consistent with what has been learned in other domains, such as in developing measures of command and control for the Defense Department (Johnson and Levis, 1988, 1989; Green and Johnson, 2002). Our measures are also consistent with a large body of RAND work on capabilities-based planning (Davis, 2002).

on the one hand and, on the other, measures that, while they may be easily measured, are actually poorly linked to effectiveness.

Reliable. Reliable measures will always have a consistent, easily interpreted relationship with an improvement in the intended outcome, whether it is increasing or decreasing in the measure. Such measures cannot be "gamed," will not create perverse incentives, and will usually have an intuitive meaning. Measures that do not meet this criterion can be counterproductive. To illustrate the point, a conceptual model might suggest the importance of thwarting illegal crossings of some stretch of border. A candidate measure might be the number of miles of fence along that border. However, if illegal crossings could be easily accomplished with tunnels and ladders that thwart fences, miles of fences would have only a weak relationship to achieving the ultimate objective of thwarting crossings. Even worse, the border-control organization would be incentivized to build additional fence—even if doing so would accomplish very little.

Useful. A set of measures needs to be useful in the sense of being amenable, at least in principle, to being monitored (i.e., we must be able to generate estimates of the measure, either quantitatively or with structured qualitative methods). Significantly, the *set* of measures may be practical overall even if, for a given measure within the set, it is necessary to use proxies, to tolerate approximations, and to make do with only sporadic empirical information. Dropping a measure because it is only sometimes possible to obtain data for it might mean sacrificing soundness of the measure set and forgoing the opportunity to use data when they do become available (e.g., through intelligence).

General. Finally, if possible, the measures should be sufficiently general so that they can be used to make comparisons across modes of transportation (land, sea, and air), program types, agencies, and geographic regions. In contrast, if, for example, one agency measured intercepts of smuggling in terms of pounds or tons of substances while another reported numbers of couriers arrested, there would be a mismatch in measurement approaches, making overall assessments difficult, as well as complicating efforts to assess relative costs and benefits of resource-allocation options.

Against this background, then, let us now proceed to describe a conceptual model allowing us to focus on the core functions of the focus missions and develop appropriate measures.

CHAPTER THREE

A Conceptual Model of Border Security as a Foundation for Measurement

Our separate considerations of the drug control, illegal migration, and counterterrorism missions led us to a common conceptual model of border security. The model captures the essence of how DHS border-security efforts contribute to these three missions, and motivates a set of measures against which border-security investments should be assessed. In this chapter, we describe our conceptual model and the fundamental border-security functions of interdiction, deterrence, and exploitation of networked intelligence.

3.1   Defining Border Security as Controlling Illegal Flows

The most fundamental concept in our model of border security is the notion of cross-border *flow*, which we define as the movement of people or material across the border.

In the context of drug control, DHS is primarily concerned with the inbound flow of illegal drugs; for illegal migration, the relevant flows consist of inbound illegal migrants; for counterterrorism, they are the flows of malicious individuals, materials, or weapons that pose a terrorist threat.[1] DHS is also concerned with outbound flows of cash profits and weapons that may fuel drug-trafficking or alien-smuggling organizations. Finally, DHS is constrained not to unreasonably hinder legal flows of people or goods in the course of trying to stop illegal flows. Across the missions, we sustain the unifying view of border security as an effort to control cross-border movement, with the ultimate goal of reducing illegal flows and not (unduly) limiting legal flows (see Figure 3.1).

Illegal flows result from conscious decisions to attempt illegal crossings. These decisions are influenced by many factors, including perceptions of policies, economic conditions, and seasonal weather and climate. For example, decisions of Mexicans to migrate to the United States depend on economic conditions in the United States and Mexico; decisions by traffickers on how much cocaine to ship are influenced by the yields of coca from seasonal crops. We refer to the number of people with the propensity to cross illegally because of factors exogenous to border-security efforts as *Potential Flow*.[2]

---

[1]   Drug trafficking and immigration are naturally discussed in terms of continuous flows of people and material, but terrorism is typically discussed in terms of hypothetical discrete border-crossing events. When dealing with the counterterrorism mission, we interpret *flow* in a correspondingly different way.

[2]   In the context of smuggling, *Potential Flow* also refers to the amount of material being carried, not the number of people.

Figure 3.1
Conceptual Model of Border Security

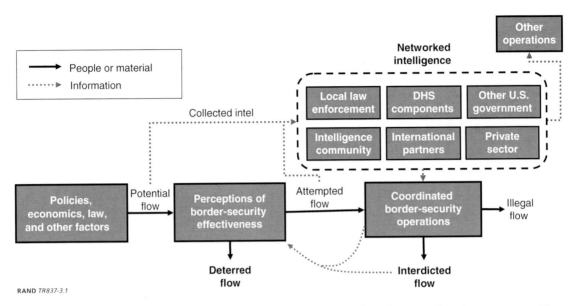

RAND TR837-3.1

The actual volume of flow may be less than potential flow because border-security efforts further influence decisions to cross the border illegally. If a migrant, drug smuggler, or terrorist believes that the effectiveness of border-security efforts make it too difficult or costly to cross the border, he or she may be deterred from doing so. *Deterred Flow* is the corresponding reduction of flow. What remains is the *Attempted Flow* at borders.

Attempts to cross the border face a variety of border-security operations. These operations are the result of collective actions of DHS components, local law enforcement, the intelligence community, other U.S. government agencies, international partners, citizens, and the private sector. To be effective, these actions must establish *Networked Intelligence* that collects information about Potential and Attempted Flows, share that information, and act on the information in a timely manner.

These coordinated border-security operations intercept flow in many ways. They can result in disruptions before flows reach the border (e.g., on approaches in the Caribbean), at the border (e.g., along the southwest U.S. border), or after the border (e.g., at traffic checkpoints). Together, the flows that are intercepted through all of these efforts represent the *Interdicted Flow*, and what or who is not interdicted enters the United States as *Illegal Flow*.[3]

3.2   Core Functions of Border-Security Activities

The conceptual model of border security described in the preceding section highlights three core functions of DHS border-security operations: (1) interdiction, (2) deterrence, and (3) exploitation of networked intelligence. The specifics of each of these functions for the focus problems are discussed in Chapter Four. However, it is useful first to understand the functions

---

[3]   As a practical matter, it could be a bit arbitrary whether border crossers arrested by local or other-federal-agency officials would be counted as "interdicted" or as arrested after successful illegal flow. We do not attempt to sort out these matters in this report. The point of the figure is merely that a system perspective needs to be taken.

generally and to consider how and why alternative border-security investment options should be assessed for performing them.

3.2.1 Interdiction

The most direct and perhaps the most important border function is interdiction. The ultimate outcome of interdiction capability is who or what penetrates the border without interdiction, and this suggests assessing the effect of investment options on the size or significance of Illegal Flow. However, Illegal Flow alone tells only part of the story, because the observation of minimal Illegal Flow can be explained either by an effective border-security system or by low Potential or Attempted Flows. Measures of Interdicted Flow are similarly incomplete and potentially misleading, as impacts on the measure can be similarly explained either by border security or by changes in Attempted Flow. At first glance, a measure of *interdiction rate* might appear to address this lack of context, by reflecting the percentage of attempted flow that is interdicted.[4] However, even an interdiction rate of 90 percent is poor if the resulting Illegal Flow is unacceptable. More generally, even if the border-control system is very effective technically and procedurally, the ultimate outcome may well depend on the magnitude of the challenge—e.g., whether Attempted Flow is measured in tens, thousands, or millions (e.g., of people, pounds of drugs).

Measures of Attempted Flow can provide this missing context but will typically depend on factors far beyond the influence of border-security efforts (notwithstanding some deterrence effects, discussed in the next section). For example, a sufficiently great consumer demand for drugs will increase the Potential (and therefore Attempted) Flow of narcotics, or an economic recession may cause growers to cut back on the use of migrant workers and decrease Potential Flow of migrants. Thus, we conclude that using Illegal Flow, Attempted Flow, Interdicted Flow, or Interdiction Rate in isolation is insufficient to appropriately assess the impact of an investment in interdiction capability.[5]

As described further in Chapter Five, to fully capture interdiction outcomes, we recommend measuring both Interdiction Rate and Attempted Flow.[6] Interdiction rate is a natural measure: It is intuitive and is meaningful over a wide range of conditions (i.e., different numbers of attempts). Moreover, it is *sound* in the sense that increasing Interdiction Rate constitutes an improved interdiction capability regardless of the Attempted Flow (even absent progress toward national policy objectives). Also, interdiction mechanisms often work in ways that relate directly to percentage of successes. For example, detection probabilities are often

---

[4] Here we refer to the percentage of attempted illegal crossings that are interdicted, not the percentage of individuals that is interdicted. Because some illegal border crossers attempt many times before successfully entering the United States, it is also useful to estimate how many individuals are coming and how often they attempt. Doing this would lead to a different estimate of interdiction rate (i.e., per person as opposed to per attempt) and require assessment of the distribution of number of attempts that individuals make. The latter piece of information may be useful for better understanding of decisionmaking by illegal border crossers.

[5] In the program-evaluation context, CBP tracks interdicted flow migrants for the White House Dashboard (DHS, 2009a). Illegal Flow is an elusive quantity, because successful border crossers are not usually detected; Illegal Flow is the figure on which we focus to estimate the size of the illegal immigrant community. Attempted Flow is similarly elusive, though the USCG has set a precedent for using Consolidated Counterdrug Database estimates of Attempted Flow to measure interdiction rate; the percentage of drug flow intercepted and migrant interdiction rate are included in the fiscal year 2009 USCG Government Performance Results Act (Pub. L. 103-62) measures (DHS, 2009a).

[6] Given any two of Attempted Flow, Illegal Flow, Interdicted Flow, or Interdiction Rate, the other quantities can be calculated.

limited by the fraction of time that human or technical sensors cover given areas. Finally, used together, Attempted Flow and Interdiction Rate can provide a complete and understandable picture of the effectiveness of border-security systems, as in, "Well, the defense system improved remarkably last year, illegal crossers were successful only 20 percent rather than 40 percent of the time. However, because the number of attempts increased by a factor of two, the number of illegal crossings was about the same."

3.2.2 Deterrence

Deterrence is a very real and observable phenomenon known in all walks of life. Typically, defensive systems, such as border security, cannot be perfectly effective (i.e., achieve a 100-percent interdiction rate). Indeed, realistic figures will often be *far* lower. In the real world (which includes concerns about economic activity, normal social functions, civil rights, and foreign affairs), resource and other constraints imply that not all portions of the border can be monitored at all times; not all potential crossers can be interrogated at length so that agents can "sense" a problem; not all potential crossers can be scanned and undergo personal body checks; not all documents that appear valid can be exposed to in-depth checks; not all physical items can be fully scrutinized with a range of detectors; and so on. To make things worse, even if the interdiction rate is very high, a defense system can be overwhelmed if the number of challengers is high enough.

As a practical matter, then, successful border security will depend heavily on the capability to deter attempts at illegal border crossings.[7] Fortunately, there is evidence of deterrent effects in many domains. For example, one explanation of crime-rate decreases in a city could be the deterrence created by a more efficient police force (Sampson and Cohen, 1988). In a domain related to border security, extensive interviews with Caribbean drug smugglers, as well as access to drug-interdiction data, allowed researchers to document a nonlinear effect in which even a rather modest probability (10 percent) of being interdicted and punished harshly caused a dramatic drop-off in attempts to smuggle by the routes in question.[8] Because of differences in the punishments and incentives associated with other forms of illegal border crossings, the existence of a similar nonlinear response would need to be demonstrated. Such empirical social science is relatively unusual, but, in cases in which it exists, it confirms and rather dramatizes the potential value of deterrence. Figure 3.2 shows our own schematic of the generic effect for cases in which criminals weigh a choice of which options to choose for criminal activity that yields finite benefits if they are successful.

Thus, conceptually, investment alternatives should be assessed for deterrent effects on Attempted Flow. In the forward-looking context of planning, assessing impact on Attempted Flow would require models that represent (1) the decision calculus of individual smugglers and their leaders, including an understanding of how interdiction capabilities affect the value and likelihood of salient outcomes of attempting to cross the border; (2) market effects, including competition among smugglers; and (3) whatever specific capability is represented by

---

[7] Deterrence features in recent statements of CBP and U.S. Border Patrol strategy (CBP, 2009). Deterrence outcomes were also mentioned in our conversations with ICE Office of Investigations and USCG.

[8] See work by the Institute for Defense Analyses on the subject (Anthony, 2004). The smugglers, of course, did not "reform" and become honest, law-abiding citizens. They looked for substitute routes or substitute lines of business. It is typical in many deterrent functions that the problems may be deflected or delayed rather than eradicated. However, the effects of deterrent functions can be cumulative.

Figure 3.2
Illustration of the Nonlinear Benefits of Deterrence

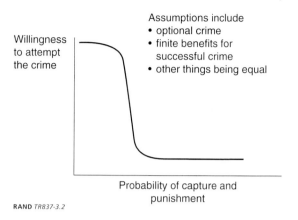

RAND *TR837-3.2*

investment alternatives. Although models representing these factors can be quite helpful and insightful, their predictions will typically be highly uncertain. Exploratory analysis methods can generate useful conclusions in some cases despite uncertainty, but accurate and reliable prediction is not in the cards. It follows that model-based calculations would not provide reliable measurement of deterrence effects.

Since it is essential to improve deterrence as part of the border-control mission, but measuring degree of success accurately is very difficult, what can be done to plan and manage? The answer, as in many domains, is in part to depend on defining and measuring *adherence to good practices*. Much is known about the factors that contribute to deterrence, even if their accurate quantitative significance—either individually or in combination—is more speculative or can be established empirically only over a lengthy period of time.[9]

Empirically supported social science can contribute by identifying the factors that affect decisions to cross illegally and that can be productively shaped by border investments.[10] For example, interviews with people captured while attempting to smuggle drugs indicate that their decisions of when and where to cross are affected by, among other things, their perceptions of the likelihood that they will be caught, the penalties for being caught, and the rate at which shipments of money from drug sales are interdicted as they are sent out of the United States. All else being equal, efforts that affect these factors will produce a greater deterrent effect than those that do not.

It should therefore be possible to define border-security practices that would almost surely contribute usefully to deterrence, to implement those practices, and to measure adherence. It should also be possible for independent assessors to evaluate from time to time whether the practices are sufficient (according to the best understanding available from experts, including law-enforcement agents) or whether there are serious holes that need to be filled with

---

[9] An obvious example here is the firm requirement that pilots actually use checklists. That can be enforced, and there is good reason to believe that doing so pays off. Some emergency rooms now enforce use of checklists for, e.g., treatment of patients who may have heart-disease symptoms.

[10] Recent theoretical work on deterring terrorist acts is relevant to this discussion (Morral and Jackson, 2009; Davis, 2009b).

additional practices. The same assessors could evaluate whether some of the practices are simply not worth the effort, cost, or side effects.

Postulating this ability to define and assess adherence to good practices may seem a stretch, and, to some extent, it is. However, consider the importance of analogous methods in other walks of life. Public-health codes, construction codes, and publicity about best medical practices have all proven quite valuable over time even though it is seldom possible—especially at the beginning—to establish neat and accurate quantitative relationships about what they accomplish. The belief is more that they work in the right direction and do not pose excessive cost or inconvenience.

As with interdiction, deterrence capability can be measured separately for different modes of transport and geographic regions because the importance of factors that affect decision making is likely to vary for different groups as well as across these dimensions.

3.2.3 Networked Intelligence

One of the unexpected results of our study was recognition of the importance of networked intelligence in elaborating objectives for and measuring effectiveness of border security.[11] This came about for many reasons.

First, all of the focus missions are best understood in national terms: Border security contributes significantly to several high-level national objectives, but results depend sensitively on interactions with and the performance of other federal and local agencies, as well as economic and demographic conditions outside of DHS's control.

Second, national-level effectiveness depends not just on individual component or agency effectiveness but also on components' ability to share information and work collaboratively, i.e., to network. This is perhaps most obvious with respect to preventing terrorism, in that individuals might enter the country who are vaguely suspicious but who cannot reasonably be arrested at the border. Responsibility for follow-up then transfers to, e.g., the Federal Bureau of Investigation (FBI). However, the FBI's ability to follow up—either immediately or when further information emerges—might depend critically on information collected *and effectively transferred* by border agencies to the FBI. The word "effectively" is key because all agencies are deluged with data. The 9/11 Commission's report dramatized the consequences of ineffectiveness: It is not that information for apprehending the perpetrators did not exist, but rather that the dots were not connected and the relevant agencies did not cooperate well (National Commission on Terrorist Attacks upon the United States, 2004).

Third, national-level law enforcement also depends on the effectiveness of the justice system, including the ability to convict and punish. That, in turn, often depends on authorities being able to construct an extensive, fact-based story of criminal behavior from which, cumulatively, guilt can reasonably be inferred by a jury.

Fourth, the nature and quality of information collected by border-security components, the consistency with which it is collected, and the effectiveness with which the data are both transferred to national databases and—where appropriate—highlighted in cross-agency actions, are leverage points for improved national-level effectiveness, especially in relation to terrorism- or drug-related functions. Border-security efforts sometimes will query detected

---

[11] It might be argued that having good networked intelligence is subordinate to the functions of interdiction and deterrence. However, border control's intelligence contributes to other national missions, such as internal law enforcement generally. Furthermore, it is important enough that it needs to be highlighted.

travelers against data sets of known or suspected terrorists or criminals. This is especially relevant at ports of entry, ports of egress in some modes, and in cases in which border enforcement detains an illegal crosser. In other settings, border-enforcement agencies collect as much information as possible on individuals, their conveyances, license plates, accounts, and other records of persons detained for crossing illegally but for whom no prior records exist. The same is true in the maritime regions when individuals are arrested for illegal drug smuggling or illegal migrant smuggling. The collected information can become future tactical intelligence (and used in prosecutions) if the detained person becomes involved in criminal or terrorist functions at a later date. Discussions with component agencies indicate that this is an important capability to measure. Technologically, it is even possible to tag individuals so that subsequent surveillance within the United States (or an other country) is possible.[12]

The effectiveness of networking can be increased by training, education, technology, and exercises, and can also be measured. These measurement issues and approaches to addressing them are discussed further in Chapters Five and Six.

3.3   Identifying Measures for Border-Security Functions

To identify measures for the fundamental functions, it is useful to first consider them within the context of the hierarchy presented in Figure 2.1 in Chapter Two. In this framing, each of the fundamental functions (i.e., interdiction, deterrence, and networked intelligence) becomes a means to achieving a policy goal.

In this manner, the functions of interdicting and deterring illegal flow and contributing to networked intelligence make up the capability block for evaluating the contributions that border-security efforts make to each focus mission. They are not, however, the only criteria against which border-security efforts must be judged. When evaluating alternative approaches to border security, it is necessary to also evaluate their costs, risks, and possible unintended consequences. These unintended consequences include potential negative side effects that the approaches may have on achieving other policy goals, perhaps outside the scope of border security, program risks, and program costs. Figure 3.3 illustrates how each of these factors relates to focus missions in the example of preventing drug smuggling.[13]

Side effects of border-security efforts could extend beyond issues generally considered border security or even the responsibility of DHS.[14] For example, efforts to increase border security may be unacceptable if they also impose delays on legitimate trade or travel. As another example, the Western Hemisphere Travel Initiative was intended to increase the ability of border-security agencies to manage cross-border travel. However, implementation of the initiative had to balance concerns that other North American countries (particularly Canada) had about how the new rules would affect economic development and cross-border trade. If implemented

---

[12] It is noteworthy that one of the highest-priority targeted killings in Afghanistan was accomplished by releasing the brother of a leader from prison and following his movements until the opportunity arose for striking that leader (Wilner, 2010).

[13] The appropriateness of lower-level objectives, such as "limit program costs," is more evident if the top-level objective is seen as mere shorthand for "secure U.S. borders confidently without unreasonable negative side effects and at reasonable cost."

[14] A fuller treatment would include the lower-level objective of finding synergies and providing for upside potential. We omit these for simplicity.

Figure 3.3
Hierarchical Relationships Among Objectives Inferred by Fundamental Border-Security Functions

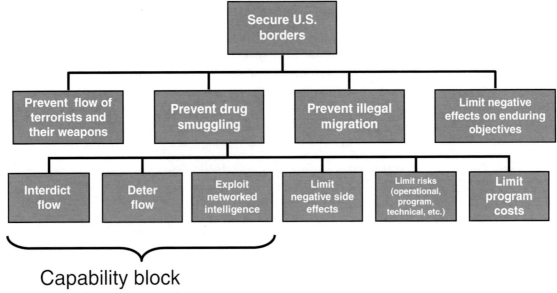

RAND *TR837-3.3*

poorly, it would have been possible for this program to improve security but possibly hinder trade and diplomatic relations with Canada.

Similarly, the manner in which a program is implemented poses different types of risks to border agencies. For example, recent efforts to increase security of the southwest U.S. border in response to drug-related border violence had the potential to reduce drug traffic and immigration traffic. However, these programs also increased risks to the border patrol by placing more personnel in a hostile environment.

Finally, not all border-security measures have the same costs. Therefore, it is important to consider program cost at the same level as both the capability block and objectives related to program risks and side effects.

CHAPTER FOUR

Contributions of Border Security to Drug Control, Counterterrorism, and Illegal Migration

In this chapter, we use the concepts of Chapter Three to describe how the fundamental functions of border-security efforts contribute to focus missions of drug control, counterterrorism, and illegal migration control.

4.1 Border-Security Contributions to Drug Control

4.1.1 National Drug Control Policy and Capabilities

The border-security mission of preventing illegal drug smuggling contributes to the broader goals outlined in the National Drug Control Strategy (ONDCP, 2009):

- stopping initiation
- reducing drug abuse and addiction
- disrupting the market for illegal drugs.

Achieving these national goals requires a breadth of functions that include treatment, prevention, domestic enforcement, and source-country control—in addition to border security. As a result, executing the national drug-control policy requires coordination among numerous U.S. government agencies, including DHS.

The role of border security can be understood better by thinking about overlapping aspects of the phenomenon. The *demand for drugs* is affected by education, treatment and incarceration of addicts, punishment for usage, and the price charged for drugs, among other things. *Supply* is affected by the profitability of drug trading and such disincentives as risk. Some kinds of risk merely result in tactical changes, which may drive up the price charged but do not really affect incentives. Other kinds of risk, such as direct threats to drug leaders of incarceration, having their financial assets frozen, and having their travel and residency locations severely limited, are disincentives that may deter activities—perhaps causing a scale-down of attempted traffic or a shift to other forms of crime. Border control can affect operational risk, forcing tactical changes that at least add cost and reduce demand, and that may be so troublesome as to have a deterrent effect. Border control can also affect risk to leaders, which can have a deterrent effect.[1]

---

[1] These overlapping processes are discussed in the drug-control literature, including in a RAND study of a system-dynamics nature (Everingham and Rydell, 1994; Rydell and Everingham, 1994).

There is an extensive body of literature examining such issues and models. A thorough review of this literature is beyond the scope of this document. However, we conclude from our review that achieving Office of National Drug Control Policy (ONDCP) objectives will likely require a portfolio of capabilities for many functions, including border security. Thus, DHS investments in border security should be assessed for contributions to, but not the actual achievement by itself of, ONDCP objectives. Moreover, good measures should highlight circumstances in which DHS contributions—or their significance in the larger context—depend on nonborder strategies or non-DHS agencies. Such measure sets will necessarily relate to other-agency efforts (see the next two sections and also Chapter Six).

4.1.2 Contributions of Interdiction, Deterrence, and Networked Intelligence to Drug Control

There are three main outcomes of border security that contribute to preventing drug smuggling; they result from the fundamental border-security functions of interdiction, deterrence, and networked intelligence.[2]

Interdiction capability contributes the first and perhaps the most direct outcome of border security for drug control: intercepting drugs before they reach illegal drug markets. Although it is clear that border security is a very important part in any strategy for controlling illegal drug use, only sometimes will marginal changes in interdiction capabilities be the most effective means of improving achievement of ONDCP objectives. This is because, e.g., (1) the replacement costs that drug-trafficking organizations incur to accommodate cocaine interdictions may be negligible relative to the total cost of drugs to users and to drug-trafficking organizations' profits (Reuter et al., 1988) and (2) there are often alternative (e.g., domestic) sources of production that can satisfy the demand (as is the case for marijuana and methamphetamine) (National Drug Threat Assessment, 2009).

Deterrence capability contributes the second, less direct, but perhaps more significant outcome: increasing the risks and costs of drug smuggling. In general, increased risks and costs can have one of two effects on the behavior of smugglers: Either smugglers are deterred by the increased risk of being caught, or they change their behavior in ways that make smuggling more costly, less profitable, or more vulnerable to interdiction (Decker and Chapman, 2008). In fact, there is evidence to support claims that some previous border operations have deterred some smugglers and caused others to use different routes or tactics; see, for example, Crane (1999) and Anthony (2008). Furthermore, in our discussions, DHS components supported the idea that an outcome of border functions is increasing the risks and costs of smuggling.

The networked-intelligence capability contributes the final outcome of border security for drug control: contributing intelligence for use by the broader drug-control community. Intelligence collected by CBP, USCG, or ICE may aid other federal agencies or state and local law enforcement in drug-control operations. For example, information garnered from interdicted drug shipments or smuggler interrogations may provide information relevant to source-control operations conducted by Joint Interagency Task Force South or to domestic enforcement operations of the U.S. Drug Enforcement Administration and FBI. In fact, whether or not DHS

---

[2]   Note that DHS also has capabilities that contribute to preventing drug smuggling but cannot be reasonably associated with border security. For example, DHS may have a role in freezing financial assets of drug-trafficking-organization leaders or in limiting the legitimate travel of wanted smugglers. We exclude these other capabilities from our conceptual model of DHS border-security capabilities that contribute to drug interdiction.

intercepts any drugs or increases risks to smugglers, simply having an awareness of cross-border flows contributes to a national intelligence picture and, as a result, might facilitate other drug-control functions. Our discussions with CBP, ICE, and USCG confirmed the importance of contributing to networked intelligence.

4.1.3 Non-DHS Agencies and Factors on Which Border-Security Outcomes Depend

As evident in the previous descriptions, the significance of DHS mission outcomes may depend on non-DHS agencies. The examples discussed in the preceding section illustrate how DHS efforts can be dependent on other-agency efforts at the operational level. However, the effect that DHS efforts have on achieving ONDCP policy objectives can also depend on efforts of other agencies. For example, a 90-percent smuggler interdiction rate may not increase risks to smugglers if U.S. Department of Justice court capacity or penalties preclude smugglers from bearing any significant consequences. More generally, whether DHS performs well or performs poorly, the United States may achieve limited progress toward ONDCP objectives without complementary contributions of other agencies.

Finally, we expect border-security effectiveness to depend on a number of external factors. It is easy to see how all three outcomes might depend on the demand and supply for drugs, the type of drug being shipped, terrain and climate conditions, and smuggler counterintelligence functions. Factors such as these are beyond DHS control, and their effects should be accounted for when measuring the contributions of border security.

4.2   Border-Security Contributions to Counterterrorism

4.2.1 National Counterterrorism Policy and Capabilities

The complexity of the counterterrorism mission is well recognized, as is the range of capabilities that can be brought to bear on the problem. The 2006 National Strategy for Combating Terrorism (NSC, 2006) illustrates the variety of short-term and long-term objectives involved in combating terrorism (see Table 4.1).

Short-term objectives are directed at disrupting terrorist planning and operations as well as hindering the ability of terrorist groups to achieve strategic goals of controlling national governments (see Table 4.1). Long-term objectives are directed at combating the roots and ideologies of terrorism and building capabilities within international coalitions to combat terrorism.

These national objectives involve influencing why people become terrorists (Helmus, 2009), how terrorist groups generate and maintain support (Paul, 2009), and how terrorist groups learn and plan (Cragin, 2007; Bonomo et al., 2007; Jackson et al., 2005, 2009). In the

Table 4.1
Objectives from the 2006 National Strategy for Combating Terrorism

Objective Type	Objective
Short term	• Prevent attacks by terrorist networks. • Deny weapons of mass destruction to terrorists and rogue states. • Deny terrorists the support and sanctuary of rogue states. • Deny terrorists control of any nation.
Long term	• Win the war of ideas by advancing effective democracy. • Promote international coalitions and partnerships. • Enhance government counterterror infrastructure and capabilities.

SOURCE: NSC (2006).

short term, success is defined by successfully disrupting terrorism (Jackson et al., 2009). In the long term, success involves ending a terrorist group's ability to sustain itself (Gvineria, 2009; Jones and Libicki, 2008).[3]

Achieving these goals requires a concerted effort focusing on domestic security, military capabilities, economics, law enforcement, intelligence, and diplomacy. With this broad set of required capabilities, DHS and its border-security agencies are but one constituency in a truly interagency mission.

Measuring these national objectives could be quite difficult. Possible measures could be the number of terrorist attacks or consequences of terrorist attacks. These measures are not perfectly reliable, because, even if a terrorist group was not attacking, it could be successfully recruiting members with knowledge of weapons of mass destruction or obtaining weapon-of-mass-destruction technologies.

Other subsidiary measures might better reflect the broader success of national policies on combating terrorism. For example, estimates of the membership of terrorist organizations or qualitative estimates of the capabilities of terrorists to conduct attack scenarios could provide indications of how counterterrorism efforts are influencing risks from terrorism.

Although these measures may be more reliable measures of national counterterrorism policies, they are not reliable measures of the contributions made by border security. Because terrorist groups can recruit and train members inside or outside the United States without necessarily crossing a border, the effectiveness of border-security efforts could have little relationship with measures like terrorist groups' membership or technical capability. Instead, to develop sound and reliable measures of the contributions of border security to counterterrorism, it is necessary to look to the fundamental capabilities of interdiction, deterrence, and networked intelligence that are part of the conceptual model in Chapter Three.

4.2.2 Contributions of Border Interdiction, Deterrence, and Networked Intelligence

The principal contributions that border security makes to counterterrorism relate to preventing certain kinds of terrorist attacks dependent on flows into the country of people or materials. These contributions can be illustrated by considering what opportunities exist to disrupt terrorist attacks while they are being planned and orchestrated.

Through a number of planning efforts, DHS and its components have developed detailed planning scenarios of terrorist events (DHS, 2006). Each of these scenarios has been deconstructed into attack trees that are useful for considering how DHS border-security programs contribute to terrorism security efforts. In their most generic form, these attack trees specify dimensions of attack scenarios with respect to building the terrorist team, identifying a target, and acquiring a weapon (see Figure 4.1). This decomposition of attack planning provides a structure around which to consider how interdiction, deterrence, and networked intelligence contribute to preventing terrorist attacks and, thus, why it is relevant to measure these functions.

DHS border-security efforts focus on interdiction of terrorist team members and weapons or weapon components when they cross U.S. borders. Examples of initiatives that are intended to enhance these capabilities include the Secure Border Initiative, the acquisition of Advanced Spectroscopic Portals for nuclear detection, the Secure Communities Initiative, and US-VISIT.

---

[3] A number of these references appear as chapters in a single book (Davis and Cragin, 2009), a RAND critical review of the scholarly social science bearing on counterterrorism.

**Figure 4.1
Notional Decomposition of Terrorist Attacks Reflected in DHS National
Planning Scenarios**

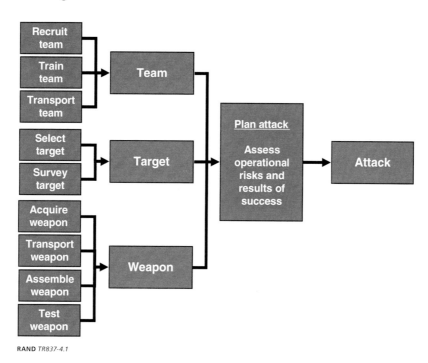

RAND *TR837-4.1*

In addition, it is often pointed out that, when border-security measures are perceived to be effective, terrorists groups may be deterred from attacking in particular ways, or possibly from attacking at all. This could result from awareness of what type of surveillance is occurring or the capability of interdiction systems. In either case, *deterrence* refers to the judgment of terrorists that they will not be successful, leading them to choose another course of action.

Finally, many border-security initiatives also contribute information to the national networked-intelligence picture. For example, the Secure Communities Initiative has implemented new capabilities to allow a single submission of fingerprints as part of the normal criminal arrest and booking process to be queried against both the FBI and DHS immigration and terrorism databases. This effort makes it easier for federal and local law enforcement to share actionable intelligence and makes it more difficult for terrorists to evade border-security efforts.

4.2.3 Non-DHS Factors on Which Border-Security Outcomes Depend

The terrorist threat that border-security efforts must counter will be significantly influenced by the effectiveness of security, economic policy, military, diplomatic, and intelligence efforts targeting other aspects of terrorism. If terrorists overseas are able to acquire significant quantities of weapon material or establish advanced counterintelligence capabilities, attack plans may easily overwhelm border-security efforts. If terrorists are successful at recruiting and building networks within the United States, border-security efforts may never get the chance to interdict attacks.

Similarly, the perceptions that terrorists have about the difficulty of entering the country could influence decisions of how to organize and plan attacks. If borders are viewed as porous and open, terrorist groups can be expected to take advantage of this vulnerability. To the extent that border security is seen as presenting barriers to terrorist planning (especially barriers that include substantial operational uncertainty), efforts will create a deterrent effect that could lead terrorists to shift to attacking interests outside the United States or attacking in different ways.

The extent to which border security will be effective at both interdicting and deterring terrorists will itself depend on a number of contextual factors, including the following:

- material being smuggled: Is it possible to detect the material using noninvasive means (e.g., with nuclear detectors)?
- mode of travel: Will crossings be via air, land, or sea?
- environment and terrain: Will crossings occur during times when and at places where border security benefits from good visibility or poor visibility?
- U.S. intelligence capabilities: Do expenditures on intelligence collection and analysis afford border security the ability to anticipate terrorist incursion attempts?
- terrorist counterintelligence capabilities: Do terrorists have enough understanding of border-security tactics and techniques to be able to avoid them and to do so with considerable confidence? The answer to this, of course, will depend on the visibility and predictability of border-security systems and procedures.

The measures used for evaluation of border-security efforts must be able to reflect some of these dependencies and factors that moderate the effectiveness of border security.

4.3   Border-Security Contributions to Preventing Illegal Migration

4.3.1 National Immigration Policy and Capabilities

The border-security mission of preventing illegal migration contributes to achieving broader national goals and objectives of immigration policy. A recent CBO study (CBO, 2006) describes the goals of U.S. immigration policy to (1) reunite family members living in the United States; (2) admit workers with specific skills and to fill positions in occupations deemed to be experiencing shortages; (3) provide refuge for people who face the risk of political, racial, or religious persecution in their country of origin; and (4) ensure diversity by providing admission to people from countries with historically low rates of immigration to the United States.[4] Enforcing immigration laws and executing immigration policy require efforts to facilitate legal immigration and to prevent illegal immigration. Border security is a mechanism for enforcing immigration laws with the goal of preventing illegal migration.

Different ways to manage or control immigration can be interpreted in the context of different theories of how and why immigration occurs. Various theories explain immigration—for example, as a migrant's calculated reaction to wage differences, as a strategy for families to reduce risk of unemployment by distributing members across labor markets, as a natural consequence of global economic integration, and as the cumulative result of individuals joining previously emigrated friends and family (Massey, Durand, and Malone, 2003). One theory of how border security affects migration is that migrants employ a cost-benefit calculation when deciding whether to emigrate and that it attempts to control flow by increasing the costs of migrating illegally. Other strategies—for example, penalizing employers who hire illegal

---

[4]   There is no one government office that establishes immigration policy in the same way that ONDCP established drug-control policy. Moreover, immigration reform is a current topic of public debate. For these reasons, it is difficult to express a single, universally accepted statement of national immigration policy.

migrants or barring immigrants from social programs—operate under the same theory by adjusting costs and benefits of migration. Massey, Durand, and Malone (2003) argue that neoclassical theory has limited explanatory power and, in fact, that immigration is better explained as a "natural consequence of broader processes of social, political, and economic integration" (p. 145). This view suggests a correspondingly broader view of immigration management that includes policies of economic integration and development.

In fact, there is an extensive body of literature that examines lawful and illegal migration, and a review of this literature is beyond the scope of this document. However, we conclude from our literature review and from our conversations with DHS components that (1) border security is just one of many approaches to managing immigration; (2) as a result, DHS investments in border security should be assessed for contributions to, but not the actual achievement of, national immigration objectives; and (3) good measures of border security should highlight circumstances in which DHS contributions—or their significance in the broader context—depend on nonborder strategies or non-DHS agencies.

4.3.2 Contributions of Border Interdiction, Deterrence, and Networked Intelligence

There are three main outcomes of border security that contribute to preventing illegal migration, and they reflect fundamental border-security capabilities of interdiction, deterrence, and networked intelligence. In many ways, the outcomes mirror the drug-control outcomes, but some important differences arise that require careful consideration.

The first outcome is to intercept migrants transiting illegally across the border.[5] Migrants intercepted while transiting illegally (1) return to their source country voluntarily, (2) return to their source country involuntarily after court proceedings or coordination with their source country, or (3) disappear into the resident population while they wait without detention for a court appearance or removal. Migrants who return to their source country, under whatever circumstances, might or might not attempt illegal migration again. These different ways an interdiction might resolve distinguish illegal migration from drug smuggling.

The second outcome is to increase the risks and costs of migrating illegally. Logically, there are three ways migrants might alter their behavior as a result of increased risks and costs: (1) they are deterred from immigrating to the United States altogether, (2) they choose legal means of migrating to the United States, or (3) they adopt riskier or costlier ways of migrating illegally. The possibility of driving illegal migrants to choose legal migration alternatives further distinguishes illegal migration from drug control and terrorism. Massey (2005) describes evidence that, in fact, many Mexican migrants chose riskier and costlier alternatives as a result of increases in border enforcement due to the Immigration Reform and Control Act of 1986, Operation Blockade, and Operation Gatekeeper.

The final outcome is to contribute intelligence relevant to other U.S. government agencies or to state and local governments. Whether or not DHS interdicts any migrants or increases the risks or costs of illegal migration, border-security functions provide an awareness of illegal cross-border flows that may be useful to the state and local governments where the migrants reside or to other federal agencies. For example, the understanding of trends in illegal flows may affect how federal resources are allocated to support public services at the state and local levels.

---

[5]   There are two main ways of transiting illegally: either without documentation or with improper documentation. We do not distinguish between these categories.

4.3.3 Non-DHS Factors on Which Border-Security Outcomes Depend

Border-security outcomes may depend at an operational level on non-DHS agencies. The dependencies effectively mirror those discussed in the context of drug control and counterterrorism and reflect intelligence sharing and operational relationships with state, local, and other federal law enforcement (GAO, 2009a, 2009b). We conclude that outcomes may be helped or hindered by operational linkages that are beyond DHS control.

In addition, the significance of border-security contributions in the broader context may depend on factors beyond DHS control. For example, from the broader view of immigration policy, perhaps the ideal outcome of interdiction is that all migrants transiting illegally are returned to their source countries and do not attempt to migrate illegally again. However, border security has little impact on court capacities or source-country procedures that may lead to release of migrants who subsequently disappear into society while awaiting a court date; and DHS has even less control over whether illegal migrants "try again." Thus, even very high interdiction rates may be inconsequential if captured migrants disappear prior to removal or if removed migrants are allowed to keep trying until they are successful.

As another example, there is evidence to suggest that increasing risks and costs of smuggling may be counterproductive without practical alternatives for legal migration. For example, one paper (Massey, 2005) discusses data collected through the Mexican Migration Project to indicate that increases in border enforcement due to the Immigration Reform and Control Act, Operation Blockade, and Operation Gatekeeper pushed migrants to cross at more-remote locations, which, in turn, increased the death rate and made it less likely that they would be caught in transit. Furthermore, the increased cost of crossing illegally decreased the likelihood that a migrant would return to the source country; when successful, migrants avoid the risks and costs associated with trying again by not returning to the source country. Thus, Massey argues, the combined effect of increasing border enforcement without providing legal alternatives was to simultaneously decrease the probability of interdiction and increase the size of the undocumented population living in the United States. Although a fuller analysis of net effects would go beyond Massey's discussion and certainly beyond the scope of this report, the example illustrates how the significance of border-security outcomes may depend on nonborder contributions to achieving the goals of immigration policy.

Notably, since the U.S. Citizenship and Immigration Service oversees all lawful immigration to the United States, DHS contributes more than border enforcement to immigration. This affords DHS control over some of the linkages and dependencies on which border security depends. However, the measures developed here focus on contributions of border security to the focus problem of illegal migration.

Finally, DHS outcomes may depend on other factors beyond DHS control. Clearly, U.S. economic conditions and economic conditions of other nations may affect the supply and demand for migrant supply and, hence, the attempted flow. To the extent that migrants rely on services of guides to smuggle them illegally across the border (e.g., "coyotes"), effectiveness may depend on the tactics the smugglers employ, including the level of countersurveillance. Interdiction outcomes may depend on climate and terrain.

CHAPTER FIVE

Recommended Measures for Controlling Drugs, Immigration, and Border Crossing by Terrorists

As described in earlier chapters and as summarized in Figure 5.1, we suggest a generic conceptual model that highlights interdiction, deterrence, and exploiting networked intelligence as key functions for each of the three special missions (controlling drug smuggling, controlling illegal immigration, and contributing to counterterrorism). This chapter provides more detail and some discussion of subtleties regarding the measures themselves. For each of the three functions, it describes the measures, submeasures, and special measurement issues raised in the descriptions of the focus missions in Chapter Four. Table 5.1 summarizes this discussion.

Figure 5.1
Decomposition of Objectives and Measures for Border Security

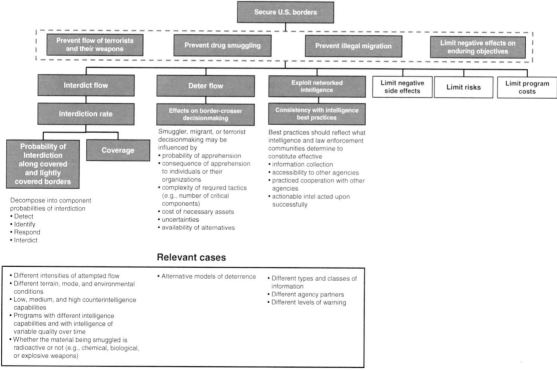

Table 5.1
Candidate Measures, Measurement Issues, and Approaches for Estimation

Objective	Measure	Submeasure or Indirect Measure	Measurement Issues and Approaches for Estimation
Interdict flow	Interdiction rate	Probability of interdiction for covered and lightly covered borders	• Where applicable, decompose into component probabilities (i.e., detect, respond, identify, and interdict). • Use empirical information (including red-team methods) and appropriately validated computer models to help support performance evaluation and planning.
		Coverage	• For terrorism, estimate subjectively the likelihood of terrorist intrusion efforts for lightly covered routes (with updates to reflect anticipated adaptations where shortcomings are observable). • For drug control, estimate the percentage of drug flow currently covered to nominal levels by border-security systems. • For illegal migration, estimate percentage of illegal migration covered to nominal levels by border-security systems. • For all, distinguish cases based on, e.g., terrain, relative knowledge, tactics.

Deter flow	Effects on border-crosser decisionmaking	Indirect measure: adherence to "best practices" for deterrence	• Best practices should reflect knowledge about deterring factors, such as
			  – probability of capture
			  – consequence of capture
			  – complexity of tactics required to succeed
			  – cost of necessary assets
			  – uncertainties
			  – availability of alternatives.
			• Importance of the factors will vary across missions, regions, and modes.
			• Decisionmakers must identify practices that are judged to have positive effects on outcomes.
			• These "best practices" should be routinely reviewed and updated and their value to improved outcomes estimated.
			• Adherence to "best practices" can be measured.
			• Program options can be assessed for value in permitting best practices.

Exploit networked intelligence	Effective collection, use, and sharing of intelligence	Indirect measure: adherence to best practices	• Best practices should reflect knowledge of DHS, intelligence, and law-enforcement communities. They should involve
			  – information collection (biographic, biometric, links)
			  – sharing with other agencies
			  – practiced cooperation with other agencies
			  – practiced operational use of networked intelligence.
			• Importance of practices may differ for drug control, counterterrorism, and illegal migration and across regions and modes.
			• Decisionmakers must identify practices that are judged to have positive effects on outcomes.
			• These "best practices" should be routinely reviewed and updated and their value to improved outcomes estimated.
			• Adherence to "best practices" can be measured.
			• Program options can be assessed for value in permitting best practices.

5.1   Measures for Interdicting Flow

The principal proposed measure for interdicting flow is Interdiction Rate, the percentage of Attempted Flow that is interdicted. Interdiction Rate is the result of three submeasures: coverage and probabilities of interdiction along the covered and lightly covered portions of the border.

This decomposition is necessary because probability of interdiction is typically very different across portions of the border and across modes.

Coverage is the percentage of flow subject to the "nominal" capabilities of the border-control system. This definition is used because large stretches of the border may be only lightly covered (e.g., less frequent patrols, lower-quality detection equipment) but also have little Attempted Flow. Thus, border fraction would not be directly meaningful.

To a first approximation (see the appendix for generalization), we refer to covered and lightly covered portions of the border. The latter should be interpreted to mean portions with less effective (although nonzero) defensive measures (and, presumably, a much smaller attempted flow).[1] A lightly covered region might, for example, be rather isolated and have very rugged or difficult terrain.

One reason to decompose the problem this way is that natural investment alternatives may trade these quantities. For example, one investment option may involve developing sensing technology to improve the probability of interdiction in a particular area. A competing investment option may expand deployments of existing resources to areas less covered.[2]

5.1.1 Interdiction Measurement Issues

Drug Control and Illegal Migration. In the drug-control and illegal-migration contexts, *coverage* would be measured as the fraction of drug flow subjected to a nominal capability of interdiction. This would require estimates from time to time of total attempted flow, including flow through routes not normally covered well. Such estimates would probably require surprise periods of intensive surveillance as well as human intelligence.

Counterterrorism. The situation is different for counterterrorism because attempted crossings will be episodic and discrete and because the issue is more one of vulnerability than actual flow. Thus, the relevant question becomes "How likely is it that we would interdict an attempted terrorist crossing?" rather than "What fraction of attempted crossings have we interdicted?" If border-control activities are somewhat unpredictable and mysterious to would-be crossers, then operators may reasonably be able to estimate whether the most-likely routes and modes of attempt are being watched to nominal levels and to turn this into a rough percentage of coverage. In practical terms, this would mean something like this:

> We think we know, from studying past practice and from consulting terrorism experts, where potential illegal migrants would be likely to attempt to cross. However, we can be wrong (especially if they know what we are doing), so we have to have *some* coverage everywhere. Still, with the proposed budget, we think that we can go about two-thirds down the list in covering the routes and modes of concern to a nominal level. Of course, our interdiction probability will be only moderate even for what we cover nominally, but it will be significant and will probably have a good deterrent effect. Before long, however, we will have to move further down the list because the terrorists will adapt if it is feasible for them to do so.

---

[1] If flow through the lightly covered portions of the border is small and the probability of interdiction is also small for such portions of the border, overall interdiction rate can be approximated as the product of coverage and probability of interdiction within the covered portions of the border.

[2] Another reason for separation is that analysis would be confusing if data applicable to regions with nominal coverage were applied to the entirety of the border and to all modes of transit equally. For example, an average probability of interdiction, calculated over the entire border, would be a number recognizable by no component or analyst other than one in headquarters.

Use of Modeling and Simulation, Empirical Data, and Other Methods. If the purpose is to evaluate performance, there is no substitute for empirical estimates of the outcomes being evaluated—either to be used directly or to be used in validating models and simulations that are used subsequently. For example, in the context of border security, it will always be necessary to develop empirical estimates of interdiction rate. The empirical information may be solid or approximate and either objective or subjective, but, in any case, it is crucial in assessing performance.

Planning for future capabilities and choosing among different ways to use current resources are different matters. Modeling and simulation can be quite valuable if there are sufficient empirical data with which to validate models, but it is infeasible or impractical to measure performance comprehensively because of the size or complexity of a system. Furthermore, if the phenomena are understood reasonably well, then modeling and simulation-based analysis (including exploratory analysis under uncertainty) can inform numerous choices even though it is not possible to validate the model and its input data precisely.[3]

This assertion may not be intuitively accepted by those who are most familiar with empirically driven work, but it is hardly hypothetical: Relevant to interdiction, for example, the U.S. Department of Defense (DoD) has a long history of using models in designing systems for detecting, acquiring, and attacking enemy targets. Although relatively small and simple conceptually, such models are sophisticated in some respects because, e.g., most surveillance systems do not permit continuous monitoring of everything. Results therefore depend on system parameters, such as overall coverage, instantaneous field of view, dwell time, repeat rate, false-alarm rate, and resolution.

Turning to interdiction in the border-security context, it should be noted that any reasonable model would reflect the fact that surveillance cannot be accomplished completely from remote air vehicles. Tunnels, for example, may be invisible to such sensors. However, surveillance can include unattended ground sensors, foot patrols, and other mechanisms, and models can estimate how effective they would be. Similarly, usual forms of sea surveillance can sometimes be thwarted by submersibles used by drug organizations, but technology opportunities exist in this domain as well, and modeling and simulation-based analysis can estimate their potential value.

Conversations with personnel from DHS components revealed several models that can contribute to decisions about how to improve probability of interdiction in particular contexts. However, new integrated models that reveal the workings and effectiveness of the entire border-security enterprise are also needed. The models should be developed to assess how changes to border-security systems and concepts of operation affect the probability of detecting different types of flows, the probability of identifying detected border crossers as illegal, the probability of physically responding to events identified as illegal, and the probability of successfully resolving the incident.[4] Once again, however, we note that even good modeling and simulation-based analysis of this sort cannot reliably estimate the absolute values of past or future performance; for that, empirical information is needed. As an example, if models were

---

[3] Exploratory analysis varies the uncertain variables simultaneously rather than one at a time as in sensitivity analysis. Even when uncertainties are substantial, it is often possible to show that one option is superior to another (but not precisely how much superior). It is also often possible to show that, because of uncertainties, a given option must be regarded as much riskier than is nominally assumed.

[4] This decomposition of interdiction into detection, identification, response, and resolution is consistent with DHS components' conceptions of border control.

superb at predicting results in covered portions of the border, it might still be the case that flow through lightly covered portions was far greater than believed because insufficient empirical effort had been made.

Chapter Six describes further implementation steps to address these measurement issues and develop models and simulations to estimate interdiction rates.

5.1.2 Measurement Cases

As discussed in Chapter Four, border-security outcomes depend on a variety of non-DHS agencies and other factors beyond DHS control. The proposed measures should be evaluated in different cases that reflect these linkages and dependencies. Examples of cases that should be considered include the level of Attempted Flow that is anticipated and characteristics of adversaries that affect the effectiveness of border-security operations. One might think of these dimensions of uncertainty as components of the diverse cases or scenarios that should be used for evaluation. Comparing the measures across such scenarios will reveal whether the benefits of an investment alternative are robust to factors beyond DHS control.

The Problem of Attempted Flow. Chapter Four described how, for drug control, counterterrorism, and illegal migration, interdiction outcomes naturally depend on the intensity of Attempted Flow. Our recommended measure of interdiction rate would seem to require a measure of attempted flow, but this is an infamously elusive quantity to measure. Estimates of attempted flow could be determined through historical intelligence (including human intelligence asking locals about relative numbers of coyotes over time), use of additional surveillance technologies, or through periodic increases in surveillance that provide statistically significant estimates of attempted flow. Although promising, efforts to obtain such data must be evaluated with respect to issues related to cost and feasibility (CFR, 2009).

When measures are used to support planning, accurate characterizations of attempted flow are less important than knowing how the border-security program performs under reasonably defined cases for different levels of attempted flow. For example, when planning, it is useful to understand how capacity of the border-control system responds to different levels of attempted flow, which may be able to respond to only one or a few detections at a given time. By necessity, computer models need to be used to estimate probability of interdiction in proposed systems as a function of scenarios and cases, including cases with different intensities and tempos of attempted flow.

Thus, models are necessary but can only go so far. Furthermore, even parametric models designed for exploratory analysis under uncertainty must be validated for that purpose (NRC, 2006). Both red-teaming and penetrator experiments that empirically probe for vulnerabilities or estimate interdiction capabilities can be used to check or inform model structures and to provide at least some data on what parameter values should be considered.

Factors That Influence Border-Security Effectiveness. The effectiveness of border-security efforts is influenced by such factors as the relative knowledge of defenses and adversaries, types of materials being smuggled, and level of activity being confronted.

Relative knowledge of both the border patrol and the adversary reflect the sophistication of U.S. intelligence and adversary counterintelligence. How well does the border patrol understand where attempts are being made? How well does the adversary understand the bordercontrol system and how it can be bypassed, tricked, or at least approached effectively? Many possible cases can be constructed for any given context. Identifying the appropriate cases for exploring capability is not trivial and deserves further discussion.

As mentioned, the three outcomes of drug control may depend on the type of material being smuggled, the demand for drugs, smuggler countersurveillance, and geographic and environmental conditions. Different configurations of these conditions (e.g., cocaine versus marijuana, radioactive material versus nonradioactive material, high versus low demand, high versus low smuggler countersurveillance) should form cases. The proposed measures should be assessed in the context of scenarios that reflect these different cases.

5.2   Measures for Deterring Flow

In principle, the capability to deter flow should be measured by the effect that DHS has on smuggler, migrant, or terrorist decisionmaking. Measuring that effect, however, is obviously very difficult. Finding and tuning a "correct" model is probably implausible. Such a model would probably be very complicated because of the many incentives at work. In the context of drug control, for example, such an assessment would require a model that reflects the dynamics of the drug market (e.g., supply-demand relationships, competition among drug-trafficking organizations) in addition to the risk calculus that smugglers employ when deciding whether and how to ship drugs. Similarly, in the context of immigration, the model would need to reflect the dynamics of the labor market and, more generally, the risk calculus that migrants employ when deciding whether and how to cross illegally.[5] For terrorism, the model would need to reflect threats imposed on would-be terrorists by foreign operations, the dynamics of terrorist networks, and the myriad of choices that terrorists have in the course of planning and executing terrorist attacks. The validity of models and associated input uncertainty would be very large.

Fortunately, simple models that reflect theories of behavior of smugglers and terrorists can be useful for identifying actions and tactics that would be expected to create deterrent effects.[6] After being identified, estimates of whether these tactics are used and the effectiveness with which they are used can become the basis of measuring whether border security is deterring flow.

This approach is consistent with a best-practices approach, however, rather than rigorous direct measurement. If best practices could be developed, then one could assess adherence to those best practices as an estimate of the deterrent effect created by border-security efforts. Also, plans should be assessed for whether they are consistent with that evidence about how to affect decisionmaking.

In thinking about "simple" models (including mere listings of factors) to help suggest deterrent measures, we note that the drug-control literature supports the idea that drug-smuggler risk is shaped by the perception of the probability of capture, smugglers' understanding of the consequences of capture, the consequence of the capture to drug-trafficking organizations, the complexity of tactics that they are required to employ, the cost of assets required

---

[5]   Another seemingly reasonable immigration measure is the percentage of all (legal and illegal) migrants who attempt to enter illegally, but it would have similar assessment requirements.

[6]   Examples of this can be seen in an empirical analysis of terrorism (Berrebi, 2009), which shows the value of using a rational-choice model to understand (and anticipate) terrorist actions. It is not that we understand the intricacies of terrorist thinking, but rather that terrorists often end up behaving in ways that are readily understandable—with the important provisos that we seek to understand their frame of reference (e.g., that in which the glories of martyrdom are quite real) and make allowances for such limitations of rationality as invalid perceptions (Davis and Cragin, 2009).

to smuggle, and smugglers' perception of life alternatives to smuggling (Decker and Chapman, 2008).[7] Risk is a perceived quality, shaped by an individual's perception of the likelihoods and values of choice outcomes. It is logical to expect migrant and terrorist decisions to be shaped by similar factors. However, perceptions and importance of these factors will differ among smugglers from different organizations and among smugglers transiting different types of contraband. In fact, in the context of illegal migration, findings by Cornelius and Lewis (2006) suggested that the deterrent effect of border security might be quite weak. Thus, understanding these differences will be necessary to knowing whether and how smugglers can be deterred. Chapter Six describes further implementation steps to address these measurement issues and identify best practices for achieving deterrence.

5.3   Measures for Exploiting Networked Intelligence

The capability to exploit networked intelligence should also be measured by the extent to which a program or investment alternative is consistent with established best practices of networked intelligence. Our initial research suggests that those practices are likely to include guidelines for how to collect information of different types, how to ensure that agencies within a network have and maintain access (technically) to other agencies in the network, how to practice interagency collaboration, and how to use actionable intelligence. Other examples of best practices may include standardization of data submissions for incident reporting or including queries of national watch lists and criminal databases as part of standard operating procedures. Unfortunately, these best practices are not yet well documented, and a concerted effort will be required to document what factors are most important to effective exploitation of networked intelligence. DHS components, law-enforcement agencies, and members of the broader intelligence community should contribute to such efforts.

When such best practices are available, initial measures for program evaluation may involve assessing simple checklists of whether organizations are taking steps that the law-enforcement and intelligence communities judge to be most effective. A program or component would be considered better if it is found through periodic audits to have adopted more of the best practices and to have done so in a way that makes sense (e.g., most-effective sets of practices first, rather than "easiest" sets of practices). As adoption of the early identified best practices penetrates the DHS component community, efforts to measure exploitation of network intelligence can mature to include more-thorough assessments of how well organizations are performing the best practices and validation of the best practices through case studies or other empirical methods. In the planning context, investment alternatives can be evaluated as to whether they help organizations address gaps in their adherence to these best practices.

In considering best practices, we should remember that DHS components collect different information, interact with different agencies, and use intelligence in different ways in the

---

[7]   There is a body of literature that attempts to model smuggler risk perception and to characterize the effect of interdiction on smugglers' decisionmaking. This literature provides a starting point for measuring the effect of investment alternatives on smuggler risk perceptions. Furthermore, the literature suggests that interviews with convicted smugglers may be a key data source for understanding these factors. Decker and Chapman motivate the need to distinguish between actual risk and perceived risk. Interviews with high-level smugglers indicate that they were unaware of the consequences of their conviction and of the fact that the United States could convict them of conspiracy.

context of drug control,[8] counterterrorism, and illegal migration. Accordingly, the specific best practices—or the relative importance of different practices—may differ by problem area.

Within each problem area, then, the best practices or the relevant importance of different practices may depend on the types of information in question (e.g., biometric, signal intelligence), the classification of information (e.g., secret, law-enforcement sensitive), the time sensitivity of the information relative to the action that may be required, and the domestic or foreign agencies that form the intelligence-sharing network. DHS capability to exploit networked intelligence should be assessed for each of these cases to provide transparency into how the capability depends on the uncontrollable factors.

Chapter Six describes further implementation steps to address these measurement issues and identify best practices for exploiting networked intelligence.

5.4   The Inadequacy of Capstone Measures for Evaluating Border Security

In our discussions, representatives of DHS components sometimes suggested the attractiveness of having a single measure (i.e., a "capstone" measure) for each of the three border-security problems. Having a single measure would in some ways be more desirable than using the set of measures proposed in this report, because it would presumably make the task of tracking and communicating progress toward goals simpler. Ideally, the agency and its components would have simple measures by which their performance could be judged. However, because of the many issues raised in Chapters Three and Four, we conclude that sound and reliable capstone measures for what DHS border-security efforts alone contribute to national policy problems do not exist.

The most-natural capstone measures involve *national* policy objectives (drug control, immigration, or counterterrorism). However, as we have seen, many non-DHS capabilities are needed to address these, and it would make no sense to credit or fault DHS for outcomes partly beyond its control. Thus, we recommend that border-security contributions to each of the three special problems be measured using a *set* of measures reflecting the three fundamental border-security capabilities. It would be reasonable to hold DHS accountable for performance by this set of measures.

---

[8]   The U.S. Government Accountability Office (2009a) includes a list of drug-related intelligence centers and the participating agencies.

Implementing Steps to Measure Border Security

In this report, we propose a set of measures of border security that reflects the contributions that DHS programs make toward three fundamental functions: interdicting illegal flows, deterring illegal flows, and exploiting networked intelligence (see Table 5.1 in Chapter Five). These measures were selected with four criteria in mind:

- soundness: the measures reflect what is important
- reliability: the measures are easy to interpret and are difficult to manipulate
- usefulness: the measures can be feasibly monitored
- generality: the measures can be broadly applied to DHS border-security efforts.

Soundness and reliability of the measures come from their connections to the conceptual model of border security presented in Chapter Three. To the extent that this model captures the essence of border security, the proposed measures are sound and reliable.

The application of these proposed measures to three special border-security problems (i.e., preventing drug smuggling, terrorism, and illegal migration) demonstrates that they can be generally applied to DHS border missions.

It remains for us to demonstrate the usefulness of these measures. Earlier chapters provide examples of how each proposed measure can be monitored in principle. However, in many cases, additional implementation efforts will be required.

A first step in this implementation will be to understand how data that are currently collected map to the functions of interdicting illegal flows, deterring illegal flows, and exploiting networked intelligence. With the findings of this report providing guidance on what should be measured, this could be the focus of a straightforward follow-on study about what actually is being measured.

Other steps to implement measures of the effectiveness of border-security efforts will require more-concerted analytic effort. These include the following:

- Develop a range of models to support planning (and performance evaluation, in some instances).
- Identify and exploit opportunities to estimate attempted illegal crossings.
- Translate studies of adversary decisionmaking into doctrine for deterrence.
- Identify best practices for exploiting networked intelligence.
- Use layered portfolio-analysis methods to evaluate past or ongoing border-security efforts, to evaluate forward-looking border-security options, and to relate results to the levels of success in other agencies' efforts.

The remainder of this chapter provides additional details of approaches that DHS can consider relating to each of these areas.

6.1 Developing Models of Border Interdiction to Support Planning

As in most domains of research and analysis, it is necessary to use a combination of theory and empirical information. Theory is often represented by models. Empirical information may be hard "data" of the form used by statisticians or the more qualitative observations of on-the-ground scientists. Ultimately, analysis needs to use families of tools (e.g., models, games, historical analysis) to make use of all the knowledge available.

The complexity of border environments and the multiplicity and uncertainty of border threats lead to a proliferation of scenarios. This situation makes comprehensive assessment of past and prospective performance infeasible using only empirical information, whether historical or from field tests.

Modeling and simulation offer a solution to this problem. Available empirical information can be used to validate tools for modeling and simulation. Then those modeling and simulation tools can be used to evaluate broadly the scenario space.

Modeling and simulation come in many forms, which include the following:

- simple conceptual models, which are more like frameworks (see, e.g., Davis and Cragin, 2009)
- relatively simple narrow models, such as those used by econometricians in both understanding and predicting rational-actor behavior (Berrebi, 2009)
- moderately complicated dynamic models, such as a system-dynamic drug-control simulation (Rydell and Everingham, 1994)
- relatively complicated but still-aggregated "campaign models," such as those heavily used over the years in DoD planning (e.g., THUNDER, STORM, ITEM, and the Joint Integrated Contingency Model, or JICM)[1]
- highly complicated models, such as DoD's Joint Warfare System, which has proven useful in some operational planning but not, in the view of most, for strategic planning
- high-resolution simulations, such as the Air Force's Brawler model of air-to-air combat.

The point here is that modeling and simulation span a huge space (see also NRC, 2006).

In our view, the modeling and simulation of most value for strategic-level work tend to be relatively simple, relatively low resolution, insightful, and analyst-friendly. Seeking reliable predictiveness would be a fool's errand, but seeking valid insights is quite sensible. Higher-resolution models are essential for component-level work but are poor instruments for higher-level analysis. Understanding relationships between lower- and higher-resolution models, however, is very important for all concerned.

---

[1]   Campaign models provide a strategic-level view of how the varied components of an organization can and should operate together. Such models should be bookkeepers, preventing double-counting of resources. They should allow walk-through simulations of how events would develop in well-constructed test cases so as to ensure that the various components have requisite capabilities, that command and control of some sort exists, and so on. Such models are subject to numerous deep uncertainties, but they can be valuable for integration and—when used with the methods of exploratory analysis over uncertainty—can also inform investment and other decisions (Davis, 2002).

Because models are so sensitive to the needs of those who build them, it is desirable for DHS to take the lead in building models well suited to headquarters-level analysis. That is, there should be a top-down architecture specialized to headquarters' needs. Much more-sophisticated modeling and simulation may be valuable at the component level for many other reasons (e.g., training, mission rehearsal, and command and control).

The resulting headquarters-level model should be informed by and relate well to models and tacit paradigms used by components, but that "relating" may be accomplished by periodic studies and parameter-range adjustments, rather than by assembling and maintaining a high-resolution composite model. Comprehensiveness, flexibility, agility, and top-level relevance are of utmost importance for such purposes. *Comprehensiveness* refers to the ability to reflect the full diversity of challenges and cases (albeit at low resolution). *Flexibility* relates to being able to address diverse policy-level questions. *Agility* refers to being able to respond quickly to new questions and options.

6.2   Identifying and Exploiting Opportunities to Estimate Attempted Illegal Crossings

Estimates of the number of attempted illegal crossings will be required to validate models and provide benchmarks for parameter values and threat levels. The vastness of the border and the ability of illegal crossers to evade some types of surveillance make it prohibitively expensive to obtain persistent measures of the number of attempted illegal crossings. It is also difficult to obtain accurate measures of the number of attempts using surveillance that covers only portions of approaches to the U.S. borders on a rotating basis. However, DHS should—at the outset and from time to time thereafter—direct special, focused surveillance efforts to estimating illegal activity crossing U.S. borders.

As confirmed in discussions with DHS component agencies, it is possible to obtain estimates of the number of illegal crossings of illegal migrants and drugs through such targeted use of surveillance and human intelligence.[2] It is also possible to construct estimates by pooling information. For example, the Consolidated Counterdrug Database provides an interagency consolidation of the estimated movements of drugs from South to North America. No similar interagency group currently exists to estimate the level of activity of illegal migration. However, discussions with border patrol suggested that it would be possible to generate similar estimates of the level of illegal migration through coordination of periodic surveillance efforts along the United States–Mexico border and of staging areas in Mexico, which were intended only to enhance domain awareness and not queue interdiction efforts.

In the case of counterterrorism, measurement of attempted illegal crossings would not be possible because this number would likely be very low. However, it should be possible to directly characterize vulnerabilities through well-designed red-team efforts and penetration testing that experimentally probes for vulnerabilities of border-security efforts or estimates their interdiction capabilities.

Before these efforts can progress, serious analysis is needed to generate and evaluate promising approaches to estimate attempted illegal crossings. Evaluation will need to consider the

---

[2]   In some cases, this would require heroic measures because the easiest surveillance (e.g., from aerial drones) cannot typically pick up activities in tunnels or submersible vessels. Other forms of surveillance are then needed.

cost, technical feasibility, and possible constraints related to privacy or other legal or political issues. This analysis will benefit from discussions that cross-fertilize perspectives across DHS components as well as from groups with experiences from other agencies, disciplines, or countries. Ultimately, these discussions can help DHS understand the trade-offs around the soundness and usefulness of approaches to estimating attempted illegal flow versus other candidate measures.

6.3   Translating Studies of Adversary Decisionmaking into Doctrine for Deterrence

"Measuring" or estimating the effects of deterrence is obviously difficult, especially because observable measures are affected also by policies and realities exogenous to border-security efforts. That said, much is known about deterrence,[3] and it should be possible to use relatively simple models of individual-level and organizational-level decisionmaking to inform decisions about how to improve deterrence. An analogue might be to the many instances in which rational-actor models with simple utility functions have been employed in business and government to gain insights about the likely effects of change. Recognizing new incentive/disincentive structures can significantly inform policy choices even though such modeling and analysis would probably not be very precise in predicting detailed responses by adversaries. Again, we believe that studies using relatively simple modeling and simulation and drawing on knowledge of practitioners within the components would be more useful in generating insights than would highly complex models that would likely depend on a great deal of highly uncertain information and highly dubious assumptions.[4]

DHS should translate the results of these studies into best practices for creating successful deterrents for illegal smuggling activities. Doing so will require a concerted analytic effort. Early measures distilled from this literature would likely resemble simple checklists of actions and tactics that have been demonstrated to deter illegal border crossers. To the extent that border-control agencies employ more of these techniques, tactics, and procedures, it might be presumed that they are having a stronger deterrent effect. That might or might not be a good presumption, however, depending on whether the *set* of practices reflects a system perspective and addresses all of the critical issues. Furthermore, some potential practices would likely have negative side effects and costs, and would not pay their way. Thus, developing such best practices would require serious analytic and empirical effort.

As use of such measures is adopted among border-security agencies, the estimates can be matured to include assessments of the effectiveness with which the tactics and strategies are being implemented. Such assessments would likely involve audits of practices and comparison to benchmarks for implementation across the border-security enterprise. It should also include routine reassessment of the practices, based on the best knowledge available. Over time, some practices would be added; some would be relaxed or abandoned. This reassessment is important

---

[3]   Two recent papers review much of the relevant literature and add new ideas relevant to counterterrorism, both generally (Davis, 2009b) and in the DHS context (Morral and Jackson, 2009).

[4]   In pursuing new analytic methods for counterterrorism and irregular warfare, DoD has reached similar conclusions, putting a priority on developing relatively simple and understandable conceptual models to represent knowledge that has a reasonable basis, rather than always incorporating layers of dubious detail in highly complicated models (see, e.g., a recent review of social-science knowledge, Davis and Cragin, 2009) to inform analytic work, including modeling.

to build in from the outset because new vulnerabilities will emerge, new adversary tactics will emerge as adversaries detect regularities and limitations of security, and unforeseen negative consequences of some practices will be discovered. Thus, occasional retuning will be essential.

6.4   Identifying Best Practices for Exploiting Networked Intelligence

Like deterrence, exploitation of networked intelligence is important to border security but does not currently have a formalized and quantified place in current evaluations. DHS should begin the process of identifying best practices based on evaluation of high-performing organizations that exploit networked intelligence. Furthermore, it should begin to develop measures of adherence to good practices. Like the process of identifying best practices for deterring smugglers, this too will require a concerted analytic effort.

A starting point, as described in Chapter Five, will involve pulling together lessons learned from the experience of components and of other kinds of organizations that use networked intelligence. Out of this could come relatively simple checklists (e.g., have watch lists been queried; have data been entered into national information databases), but also requirements for training, doctrine, equipment, and organization.

One concrete step, potentially of considerable value, would be to systematize "hand-over processes," such as when border-control functions identify suspicious individuals who must be permitted entry but who might bear follow-up surveillance. Data could be developed on such processes to ensure that hand-over mechanisms exist and work (including the person-to-person communications) and that data obtained at entry get into appropriate databases and are used appropriately. Developing these processes and related measures would require serious analytic effort based on operations-level realities, but appears feasible. Consider the questions "How often are people granted entry, despite some suspicions, only to disappear into the United States? How often are they tracked, or even surveilled?" Despite the subjectivity in such questions (e.g., who is "suspicious"), asking them and estimating the answers might substantially improve cross-organization coordination (a form of connecting the dots).

As adoption of the early identified best practices penetrates the law-enforcement community, efforts to measure exploitation of network intelligence can mature to include assessment of how well organizations are performing the best practices and validation of the best practices through case studies, audits, or other empirical methods.

6.5   Evaluating Border-Security Efforts Using a Layered Portfolio View

One element of our thinking in this report has been to anticipate how border-control analysis could be discussed effectively with policymakers—primarily within DHS, but also in senior cross-agency meetings. Such meetings might be, for example, to review performance of particular agencies or components or to review effectiveness of overall national efforts (e.g., in reducing drug use). The meetings might instead be about evaluating options for moving forward: for comparing different options for investment and for otherwise allocating and organizing resources. It is therefore worth considering whether the measures we suggest could be useful in any or all of these contexts and, if so, how they would be used.

A good deal of work in recent years has gone into designing analytic methods to support constructive meetings with senior leaders and, earlier, the meetings of senior staff in which options and recommendations are debated and honed.[5] Some of the lessons from that prior work are described here.

- *Value of Structural Commonalities.* If discussions can be structured in similar ways across problem areas and meetings, participants will be more able to quickly orient themselves to the particular problem of a specific meeting and engage substantively. Such regularities have long proven their value in top-level corporate meetings (where, e.g., spreadsheet-based financial summaries are discussed) and in military organizations.

- *General Value of the Portfolio Analysis Paradigm.*[6] Policymakers seldom have the luxury of reviewing options seeking to optimize by some simple criterion. Rather, it is an inherent part of strategic planning that issues must be addressed with multiple objectives in mind (some of them conflicting), with multiple instruments potentially available for use, and with major uncertainties precluding anything like "optimization." A natural way to proceed is to assess options for the "balance" that they provide across the various criteria. Are all of the critical objectives being attended to? If not, can resources be shifted somewhat so as to mitigate the more serious shortcomings without creating undue risks elsewhere? If additional funds are available, where would they be most profitably applied given the many objectives? If funds must be cut, where can they be made with fewest problems? Portfolio analysis is ideally suited to such strategic-level work.

- *Requirements for Effective Discussion.* To address such issues effectively and efficiently at senior levels, several imperatives exist that affect analysis and the display of analysis:
  - A top-level view should convey a quick sense of "balance" (or imbalance) across objectives, including effectiveness in multiple categories, risk management, upside potential, and cost.
  - It must be possible to "zoom" (i.e., to "drill down") in order to understand and debate the basis for top-level assessments (i.e., "Why does option B look so poor? We know it worked in case X"). The drill-down should result in another quickly comprehended summary, but a notch down in detail. It might, for example, show that option B does very well in one class of cases but very poorly in others; or it might show that it is very risky in several dimensions. Further drill-down might also be necessary. Although multiple and in-depth drill-downs will seldom occur in senior meetings, organizing analysis and conducting staff-level reviews in such layered structures is exceptionally powerful. Furthermore, if senior leaders can test their staff by asking penetrating questions on selected items (and if they are impressed by the results), they will have more confidence in the results and be better able to internalize the "story" emerging from the analysis.

---

[5] See, for example, Davis, Shaver, and Beck (2008), which describes generic methods developed for DoD's Under Secretary for Acquisition, Technology, and Logistics. A related portfolio-analysis tool has been developed and documented (Davis and Dreyer, 2009).

[6] This discussion of portfolio analysis relates to framing and assessing options, not to organizational structure. The senior figures in any reasonable organization can view issues through the lens of portfolio analysis, whether or not the organization has anointed "portfolio managers." Furthermore, if it is observed that certain cross-cutting issues are not being well addressed in an existing organization, those issues could be addressed with a special portfolio-analysis study applied "by overlay" rather than by changing organizational structure. In other cases, a changed permanent structure might be called for. Such matters are distinct from the analysis discussed here.

- *Representing Uncertainty and Disagreement.* Strategic-level assessments are very often uncertain, despite best efforts. The uncertainties should be understood by decisionmakers. Furthermore, and equally or more important, there will often be disagreements about priorities, the plausible effectiveness of proposed actions, and the real-world political or organizational viability of proposed actions. It is not the role of analysts to resolve such disagreements, but it is a role of analysis to acknowledge them and clarify their implications. This implies that even high-level summary analysis suitable for senior staffs and decisionmakers must reflect not just uncertainties, but the significance of different "perspectives."
- *Sophisticated Cost-Effectiveness.* In days of old, it was often claimed that options should be compared in terms of cost-effectiveness, sometimes reduced to a single measure of effectiveness divided by a single measure of cost. Strategic decisionmakers, however, need to be able to see how well a variety of objectives can be achieved as a function of cost. A single composite measure will suppress uncertainty and disagreement. A single budget number will suppress the potential value of increasing the budget and information on how serious a budget decrease would actually be. A good way to deal with these issues is with displays of the sort described in the next sections.

6.5.1 Suitability of the Proposed Border-Control Measures

The measures that we propose for border-control work are consistent with using portfolio-analysis methods as discussed in the preceding section. They provide for comprehensive, top-level views, selective drill-down, and recognition of both uncertainty and disagreement. Furthermore, they provide the building blocks for tailoring portfolio-analysis discussions to different purposes (e.g., reviews of performance within DHS versus comparison of different investment options; and reviews of national-level performance and options that involve cross-agency coordination). Figure 6.1 illustrates the kind of displays possible for the measures we have used. The top chart in this figure shows assessments relating to each of three options' effectiveness for drug control, counterterrorism, and controlling illegal immigration, and for their acceptability given possible side effects. If one wishes to know more about the assessment for immigration, one "zooms" to the middle chart, which shows that the top-level assessment is the result of considering ability to interdict, ability to deter, and ability to limit risk (e.g., operational, technical, programmatic, and socialpolitical risks). If one wishes to know more about the assessment for interdiction, then a further zoom to the lowest-level chart shows estimates for the probabilities per attempted border crossing of detection, response, and resolution.

6.5.2 Showing Relationships Between Border Security and Other Capabilities

Within DHS, the focus should ordinarily be on ensuring that DHS accomplishes the missions assigned to it. However, the Secretary also participates in national-level efforts in cooperation with other cabinet departments. It would be appropriate for her to emphasize that the various national efforts involve "system problems" and that system-level consequences of actions depend on synergy across the departments. She should advocate in support of other departments' efforts and resources where they would materially improve system-level effects. A notional example is shown in Figure 6.2. The objective is to reduce drug consumption in the United States. The first row of the table asserts that DHS is not doing as well as it should be but that—with planned changes—it expects to be doing its job well (yellow turns to green). The row as a whole says that, if the other agencies are also doing well, then the overall outcome should be good (green). However, the figure then goes on to point out ways in which outcomes

Figure 6.1
Notional Example Application of Using Portfolio-Analysis Methods to Present a Hierarchical Evaluation of Alternative Program Options for Border Security

Measures Investment Options	Prevent Terrorism Detail	Prevent Drug Smuggling Detail	Prevent Illegal Migration Detail	Balance Effects on Other Objectives Detail	Total Cost: 2010–2015 ($M) Cost Detail
Option 1					0
Option 2					800
Option 3					1500

Level 1 Measure	Prevent Illegal Immigration				
Level 2 Measure	Interdict	Deter	Use Networked intelligence	Limit Risk	
Investment Options					Prevent Illegal Immigration Score
Option 1					
Option 2					
Option 3					

Level 2 Measure	Interdict					
Level 3 Measure	Coverage (%)	Detect	Respond	Resolve	(Calc) Prob Interdiction	
Investment Options						Interdict Score
Option 1	50.00	0.30	0.50	0.70	0.05	0.41
Option 2	90.00	0.80	1.00	0.90	0.65	0.85
Option 3	95.00	0.95	1.00	1.00	0.90	0.96

NOTE: The colors red, orange, yellow, light green, and dark green are used to communicate an assessment of performance from poor to good, respectively.
RAND TR837-6.1

could still be poor even though DHS is successful. When discussing the figure, the Secretary would explain each row. For example, if education and other efforts to reduce drug demand are poor, it is implausible that drug control will work out well. If individuals apprehended by

Figure 6.2
Notional Example of How Portfolio Analysis Can Be Used to Illustrate Dependencies Among Agency Efforts to Achieve National Policy Objectives

Case	DHS Effectiveness		DOJ Effectiveness (convictions; punishment)	Efforts to Reduce Consumer Demand for Drugs	Internal Law Enforcement Against Drug Traffickers	Expected Outcome (drug consumption)
	Current	Projected				
1	Marginal	High	High	High	High	High
2	Marginal	High	High	Low	High	Low
3	Marginal	High	Low	Medium	High	Low
4	Marginal	High	Medium	Medium	High	Low

NOTE: The colors red, yellow, and green are used to communicate an assessment of performance from poor to good, respectively.
RAND *TR837-6.2*

border control (or by the FBI, etc.) are immediately released without punishment, the deterrent value of such enforcement efforts will plummet. The context imagined here is of senior leaders agreeing that coordinated efforts are necessary and supporting each others' appropriate requests for support or authority. The success of each depends on the success of all.

If the steps described in this section are taken, DHS and its components will be in a better position to discuss past performance and to provide reasoned justifications for future allocation of resources. Furthermore, they will be able to relate their efforts to those of other agencies in pursuit of national objectives.

Notes on Measuring Interdiction Rate and Coverage

The main body of this document recommends interdiction rate as a measure of the capability to interdict cross-border flows. The objectives of this appendix are as follows:

- Describe a mathematical model of the U.S. border that may facilitate computations of interdiction rate.
- Further motivate the submeasures of coverage and probability of interdiction along the covered border.
- Describe several modeling approaches and assumptions that may be useful or necessary to evaluate border-security investment alternatives.

A.1. Toward a Mathematical Model of the U.S. Border

We model the geographic border as a line segment $[0, L]$ partitioned into N segments indexed by $i = 1, \ldots, N$. Let air, land, and sea modes of transport be indexed by $j = 1,2,3$. Let A_{ij} and I_{ij} denote the attempted and interdicted flow, respectively, at segment i and across mode j; let R_{ij} denote the corresponding interdiction rate I_{ij}/A_{ij}. For drug control, the units of A_{ij} and I_{ij} may be kilograms of cocaine (or whatever drug); for immigration control, the units may be number of illegal migrants; for counterterrorism, the units should be paths that the terrorists could use to enter the United States, weighted by the priority with which it is believed they should be defended.

Both attempted flow and DHS border capabilities will naturally vary across segments and modes. For example, we expect there to be different risks and costs associated with crossing the border at different segments. Thus, drug smugglers, illegal migrants, and terrorists may favor some segments or modes over others. Moreover, due to DHS resource constraints and the sheer size of the border, there may always be differences in the quantity or quality of people, technology, or infrastructure that DHS allocates across segments and modes. Finally, different segments have different terrain and climate patterns that may be more or less conducive to cross-border transit or to border operations.

Accordingly, natural investment alternatives may be framed in terms of enhancing capability at particular segments or mode, or shifting resources from one segment or mode to another. Thus, the measures of interdiction rate should be computed for each segment and mode, and aggregated when a national view is necessary or more appropriate. Note that, in general, national interdiction rate can be calculated as a weighted linear combination of per-segment, per-mode interdiction rates. For national attempted flow

$$A = \sum_{ij} A_{ij}$$

and national interdicted flow

$$I = \sum_{ij} I_{ij} \, ,$$

the national interdiction rate R is given by

$$R = \frac{I}{A} = \frac{1}{A}\sum_{ij} I_{ij} = \frac{1}{A}\sum_{ij} I_{ij}\frac{A_{ij}}{A_{ij}} = \sum_{ij} R_{ij}\frac{A_{ij}}{A} \, .$$

This is the linear combination of per-segment, per-mode interdiction rates with the weights determined by the percentage of attempted flow crossing at each mode and segment.

The preceding discussion naturally raises the question of how to segment the border so that the measures are meaningful. DHS makes strategic trade-offs between border regions (e.g., northern border, the southwest border, the southeast coastal region). Although it may be meaningful to compare interdiction rates across regions, measurement must be at a more granular level, because attempted flow, border capabilities, and the factors that drive them are likely to vary at a lower level. At the opposite extreme, however, it is not useful to think about attempted flow or border capabilities as varying continuously (i.e., so that interdiction rate at point x could differ from interdiction rate at point x + ε for any ε), because border-control capabilities are better thought of as blocks corresponding to different assignments of tactical control, and tactical control does not vary continuously.

We recommend an approach that partitions the geographic border into the longest possible segments under the constraint that the terrain, climate, and border-control capability can be reasonably conceived as constant within each segment. For example, we would recommend measuring interdiction rate for a segment corresponding to areas assigned to the responsibility of one U.S. Border Patrol station, assuming that the terrain does not vary considerably within that area. In contrast, we would not recommend measuring interdiction at the level of U.S. Border Patrol sectors, because we know that the terrain, climate, people, technology, and infrastructure may vary within sectors. To emphasize, regional or national measures could be had by rolling up more granular measurements of interdiction rate.

A.2. Distinguishing Coverage and Probability of Interdiction Along the Covered Border

The model described in the preceding section suggests that, for any mode, interdiction rate varies in a piecewise-constant manner across the length of the border. In principle, similar improvements in national interdiction rate could be had either (1) by allocating resources to the few segments with the greatest (or most significant) attempted flows or (2) through diffuse allocations of resources across many segments. In practice, the effectiveness of these investment strategies could be very different depending on how adaptive the adversary is; after all, highly adaptive smugglers can always shift attention away from a segment with increased capability. Because smuggler, migrant, or terrorist adaptation occurs over time and may be unpredictable, more-diffuse allocations of resources may offer a way to hedge the risk of future adaptation. In contrast, concentrated build ups may be warranted when threat assessments are good.

Good national (or even regional) measures of interdiction rate must provide transparency into the inherent trade-offs between these sorts of investment alternatives. One could propose mathematically sophisticated measures of the diffusion of resources (e.g., information theoretic measures of entropy come to mind). However, we recommend a simpler approach of distinguishing submeasures of coverage and probability of interdiction along the covered border.

In theory, probability of interdiction along the covered border could be assessed at the segment level. In practice, there may be sufficient commonality between some segments that measurements at one segment may naturally generalize to another. Measurements of coverage should look across segments and be defined conceptually as the percentage of Attempted Flow that is subject to a nominal chance of interdiction. Naturally, this will require a threshold on the probability of interdiction below which a segment is not considered covered. Ultimately, this is a simplification that will need to be validated.

A.3. Modeling Approaches and Assumptions

Computer modeling may support measures of the probability of interdiction. How the models are structured may depend on what investment alternatives are being considered. For example, it may be useful to model the probability of interdiction according to a "kill-chain" of detection, identification, response, and resolution—especially when investment alternatives can be seen to operate independently on conditional probabilities of detection, identification given detection, response given identification, and so on. Other investment alternatives—e.g., new concepts of coordinated operation—might jointly affect elemental kill-chain components and might require another structure that appropriately captures their effects.

Crucially, our lowest-level measures (i.e., those based on the kill-chain model) should *not* be hard-wired into a management system. Empirical analysis of what factors drive interdiction rate will be required before necessary computer models can be designed.

Bibliography

9/11 Commission—*see* National Commission on Terrorist Attacks upon the United States.

Anthony, Robert, "A Calibrated Model of the Psychology of Deterrence," *Bulletin on Narcotics*, Vol. LVI, No. 1–2, 2004, pp. 49–64. As of March 29, 2010: http://www.unodc.org/pdf/bulletin/bulletin_2004_01_01_1_Art2.pdf

Berrebi, Claude, "The Economics of Terrorism and Counterterrorism: What Matters and Is Rational-Choice Theory Helpful?" in Paul K. Davis and Kim Cragin, eds., *Social Science for Counterterrorism: Putting the Pieces Together*, Santa Monica, Calif.: RAND Corporation, MG-849-OSD, 2009, pp. 151–208. As of March 29, 2010: http://www.rand.org/pubs/monographs/MG849/

Bonomo, James, Giacomo Bergamo, David R. Frelinger, John Gordon IV, and Brian A. Jackson, *Stealing the Sword: Limiting Terrorist Use of Advanced Conventional Weapons*, Santa Monica, Calif.: RAND Corporation, MG-510-DHS, 2007. As of March 29, 2010: http://www.rand.org/pubs/monographs/MG510/

CBO—*see* Congressional Budget Office.

CBP—*see* U.S. Customs and Border Protection.

CFR—*see* Council on Foreign Relations.

Congressional Budget Office, *Immigration Policy in the United States*, Washington, D.C., February 2006. As of March 29, 2010: http://purl.access.gpo.gov/GPO/LPS72417

Cornelius, Wayne A., and Jessa M. Lewis, *Impacts of Border Enforcement on Mexican Migration: The View from Sending Communities*, Boulder, Colo.: Lynne Rienner, 2006.

Council on Foreign Relations, Independent Task Force on U.S. Immigration Policy, *U.S. Immigration Policy*, New York: Council on Foreign Relations, Independent Task Force Report 63, July 2009. As of January 21, 2010: http://www.cfr.org/publication/20030/

Cragin, Kim, *Understanding Terrorist Ideology*, testimony presented before the U.S. Senate Select Committee on Intelligence, Santa Monica, Calif.: RAND Corporation, CT-283, June 12, 2007. As of March 29, 2010: http://www.rand.org/pubs/testimonies/CT283/

Crane, Barry, *Deterrence Effects of Operation Frontier Shield*, Alexandria, Va.: Institute for Defense Analyses, 1999.

Davis, Paul K., *Analytic Architecture for Capabilities-Based Planning, Mission-System Analysis, and Transformation*, Santa Monica, Calif.: RAND Corporation, MR-1513-OSD, 2002. As of March 29, 2010: http://www.rand.org/pubs/monograph_reports/MR1513/

———, "Representing Social-Science Knowledge Analytically," in Paul K. Davis and Kim Cragin, eds., *Social Science for Counterterrorism: Putting the Pieces Together*, Santa Monica, Calif.: RAND Corporation, MG-849-OSD, 2009, pp. 401–452. As of March 29, 2010: http://www.rand.org/pubs/monographs/MG849/

_____, *Simple Models to Explore Deterrence and More General Influence in the War with al-Qaeda*, Santa Monica, Calif.: RAND Corporation, OP-296-OSD, forthcoming.

Davis, Paul K., and Kim Cragin, eds., *Social Science for Counterterrorism: Putting the Pieces Together*, Santa Monica, Calif.: RAND Corporation, MG-849-OSD, 2009. As of March 29, 2010: http://www.rand.org/pubs/monographs/MG849/

Davis, Paul K., and Paul Dreyer, *RAND's Portfolio Analysis Tool (PAT): Theory, Methods, and Reference Manual*, Santa Monica, Calif.: RAND Corporation, TR-756-OSD, 2009. As of March 29, 2010: http://www.rand.org/pubs/technical_reports/TR756/

Davis, Paul K., Russell D. Shaver, and Justin Beck, *Portfolio-Analysis Methods for Assessing Capability Options*, Santa Monica, Calif.: RAND Corporation, MG-662-OSD, 2008. As of March 29, 2010: http://www.rand.org/pubs/monographs/MG662/

Decker, Scott H., and Margaret Townsend Chapman, *Drug Smugglers on Drug Smuggling: Lessons from the Inside*, Philadelphia, Pa.: Temple University Press, 2008.

DHS—*see* U.S. Department of Homeland Security.

Everingham, Susan S., and C. Peter Rydell, *Modeling the Demand for Cocaine*, Santa Monica, Calif.: RAND Corporation, MR-332-ONDCP/A/DPRC, January 1994. As of March 29, 2010: http://www.rand.org/pubs/monograph_reports/MR332/

Green, John M., and Bonnie W. Johnson, *Toward a Theory of Measures of Effectiveness*, presented at 7th International Command and Control Research and Technology Symposium, Quebec City, 2002. As of March 29, 2010: http://www.dodccrp.org/events/7th_ICCRTS/Tracks/pdf/105.PDF

Gvineria, Gaga, "How Does Terrorism End?" in Paul K. Davis and Kim Cragin, eds., *Social Science for Counterterrorism: Putting the Pieces Together*, Santa Monica, Calif.: RAND Corporation, MG-849-OSD, 2009, pp. 257–298. As of March 29, 2010: http://www.rand.org/pubs/monographs/MG849/

Helmus, Todd C., "Why and How Some People Become Terrorists," in Paul K. Davis and Kim Cragin, eds., *Social Science for Counterterrorism: Putting the Pieces Together*, Santa Monica, Calif.: RAND Corporation, MG-849-OSD, 2009, pp. 71–112. As of March 29, 2010: http://www.rand.org/pubs/monographs/MG849/

Jackson, Brian A., John C. Baker, Peter Chalk, Kim Cragin, John V. Parachini, and Horacio R. Trujillo, *Aptitude for Destruction*, Vol. 1: *Organizational Learning in Terrorist Groups and Its Implications for Combating Terrorism*, Santa Monica, Calif.: RAND Corporation, MG-331-NIJ, 2005. As of March 29, 2010: http://www.rand.org/pubs/monographs/MG331/

_____, "Organizational Decisionmaking by Terrorist Groups," in Paul K. Davis and Kim Cragin, eds., *Social Science for Counterterrorism: Putting the Pieces Together*, Santa Monica, Calif.: RAND Corporation, MG-849-OSD, 2009, pp. 209–256. As of March 29, 2010: http://www.rand.org/pubs/monographs/MG849/

Johnson, Stuart E., and Alexander E. Levis, eds., *Science of Command and Control: Coping with Uncertainty*, Washington, D.C.: AFCEA International Press, 1988.

_____, eds., *Science of Command and Control*, Part II: *Coping with Complexity*, Washington, D.C.: AFCE International Press, 1989.

Jones, Seth G., and Martin C. Libicki, *How Terrorist Groups End: Implications for Countering al Qa'ida*, Santa Monica, Calif.: RAND Corporation, MG-741-1-RC, 2008. As of March 29, 2010: http://www.rand.org/pubs/monographs/MG741-1/

Keeney, Ralph L., *Value-Focused Thinking: A Path to Creative Decisionmaking*, Cambridge, Mass.: Harvard University Press, 1992.

Massey, Douglas S., *Backfire at the Border: Why Enforcement Without Legalization Cannot Stop Illegal Immigration*, Washington, D.C.: CATO Institute, Trade Policy Analysis 29, June 13, 2005. As of March 29, 2010: http://www.freetrade.org/pubs/pas/tpa-029es.html

Massey, Douglas S., Jorge Durand, and Nolan J. Malone, *Beyond Smoke and Mirrors: Mexican Immigration in an Era of Economic Integration*, New York: Russell Sage Foundation, 2003.

Morral, Andrew R., and Brian A. Jackson, *Understanding the Role of Deterrence in Counterterrorism Security*, Santa Monica, Calif.: RAND Corporation, OP-281-RC, 2009. As of March 29, 2010: http://www.rand.org/pubs/occasional_papers/OP281/

National Commission on Terrorist Attacks upon the United States, *The 9/11 Commission Report: Final Report of the National Commission on Terrorist Attacks upon the United States*, New York: Norton, July 22, 2004. As of March 29, 2010: http://www.gpoaccess.gov/911/index.html

National Drug Intelligence Center, *National Drug Threat Assessment 2009*, Johnstown, Pa.: U.S. Department of Justice, National Drug Intelligence Center, 2008-Q0317-005, December 2008. As of April 25, 2010: http://www.justice.gov/ndic/pubs31/31379/index.htm

National Research Council, Committee on Modeling and Simulation for Defense Transformation, *Defense Modeling, Simulation, and Analysis: Meeting the Challenge*, Washington, D.C.: National Academies Press, 2006.

National Security Council, *National Strategy for Combating Terrorism*, Washington, D.C., September 2006. As of March 31, 2010: http://purl.access.gpo.gov/GPO/LPS74421

NRC—*see* National Research Council.

NSC—*see* National Security Council.

Office of National Drug Control Policy, *National Drug Control Strategy*, Washington, D.C.: White House, 2009. As of March 29, 2010: http://purl.access.gpo.gov/GPO/LPS6500

ONDCP—*see* Office of National Drug Control Policy.

Paul, Christopher, "How Do Terrorists Generate and Maintain Support?" in Paul K. Davis and Kim Cragin, eds., *Social Science for Counterterrorism: Putting the Pieces Together*, Santa Monica, Calif.: RAND Corporation, MG-849-OSD, 2009, pp. 113–150. As of March 29, 2010: http://www.rand.org/pubs/monographs/MG849/

Public Law 99-603, Immigration Reform and Control Act, November 6, 1986.

Public Law 103-62, Government Performance and Results Act, August 3, 1993.

Reuter, Peter H., Gordon Crawford, Jonathan Cave, Patrick Murphy, Don Henry, William Lisowski, and Eleanor Sullivan Wainstein, *Sealing the Borders: The Effects of Increased Military Participation in Drug Interdiction*, Santa Monica, Calif.: RAND Corporation, R-3594-USDP, 1988. As of April 24, 2010: http://www.rand.org/pubs/reports/R3594/

Rydell, C. Peter, and Susan S. Everingham, *Controlling Cocaine: Supply Versus Demand Programs*, Santa Monica, Calif.: RAND Corporation, MR-331-ONDCP/A/DPRC, 1994. As of March 29, 2010: http://www.rand.org/pubs/monograph_reports/MR331/

Sampson, Robert J., and Jacqueline Cohen, "Deterrent Effects of the Police on Crime: A Replication and Theoretical Extension," *Law and Society Review*, Vol. 22, No. 1, 1988, pp. 163–190.

U.S. Customs and Border Protection, *National Border Patrol Strategy*, Washington, D.C., 2009.

U.S. Department of Homeland Security, *National Planning Scenarios*, final version 21.3, Washington, D.C., 2006.

————, *Quarterly Status Report on the Department of Homeland Security's Border Security Performance and Resources: 4th Quarter, Fiscal Year 2008*, Report to the U.S. House of Representatives Committee on Appropriations Subcommittee on Homeland Security, Washington, D.C., 2008.

————, *White House Dashboard*, Washington, D.C.: White House, 2009a.

————, *Department of Homeland Security Annual Performance Report: Fiscal Years 2008–2010*, Washington, D.C., May 7, 2009b.

U.S. Government Accountability Office, *Immigration Enforcement: Better Controls Needed Over Program Authorizing State and Local Enforcement of Federal Immigration Laws—Report to Congressional Requesters*, Washington, D.C., GAO-09-109, January 2009a. As of March 29, 2010: http://purl.access.gpo.gov/GPO/LPS113364

————, *Drug Control: Better Coordination with the Department of Homeland Security and an Updated Accountability Framework Can Further Enhance DEA's Efforts to Meet Post-9/11 Responsibilities—Report to the Co-Chairman, Caucus on International Narcotics Control, U.S. Senate*, Washington, D.C., GAO-09-63, March 2009b. As of March 29, 2010: http://purl.access.gpo.gov/GPO/LPS114093

Wilner, Alex S., "Targeted Killings in Afghanistan: Measuring Coercion and Deterrence in Counterterrorism and Counterinsurgency," *Studies in Conflict and Terrorism*, Vol. 33, No. 4, April 2010, pp. 307–329.

Wilson, James Q., *Thinking About Crime*, rev. 2nd ed., New York: Basic Books, September 1983.

Wilson, James Q., and George L. Kelling, "Broken Windows: The Police and Neighborhood Safety," *Atlantic*, March 1982. As of March 29, 2010: http://www.theatlantic.com/magazine/archive/1982/03/broken-windows/4465/